D1175759

COOK ANIME

COOK ANIME

EAT LIKE YOUR FAVORITE CHARACTER—FROM BENTO TO YAKISOBA

DIANA AULT

TILLER PRESS
New York London Toronto Sydney New Delhi

An Imprint of Simon & Schuster, Inc.
1230 Avenue of the Americas
New York, NY 10020

First Tiller Press hardcover edition September 2020

TILLER PRESS and colophon are trademarks of Simon & Schuster, Inc.

For information about special discounts for bulk purchases, please contact Simon & Schuster Special Sales at 1-866-506-1949 or business@simonandschuster.com.

The Simon & Schuster Speakers Bureau can bring authors to your live event. For more information or to book an event, contact the Simon & Schuster Speakers Bureau at 1-866-248-3049 or visit our website at www.simonspeakers.com.

Interior design by Matt Ryan
Illustrations by Nero Hamaoui
Cover photography produced by Blueline Creative Group LLC.
Visit: www.bluelinecreativegroup.com
Cover photography produced by Katherine Cobbs
Cover photography by Becky Luigart-Stayner
Cover food styling by Torie Cox
Cover food styling assistance by Gordon Sawyer

Manufactured in the United States of America

5 7 9 10 8 6

Library of Congress Cataloging-in-Publication Data
Names: Ault, Diana, author.
Title: Cook anime : eat like your favorite character : from Bento to Okonomiyaki / by Diana Ault.
Description: First Tiller Press hardcover edition. | New York : Tiller Press, 2020. | Includes index.
Identifiers: LCCN 2020016343 (print) | LCCN 2020016344 (ebook) | ISBN 9781982143916 (hardcover) | ISBN 9781982143923 (ebook)
Subjects: LCSH: Cooking, Japanese. | Animated films—Japan
Classification: LCC TX724.5.J3 A95 2020 (print) | LCC TX724.5.J3 (ebook) | DDC 641.5952—dc23
LC record available at https://lccn.loc.gov/2020016343
LC ebook record available at https://lccn.loc.gov/2020016344

ISBN 978-1-9821-4391-6

ISBN 978-1-9821-4392-3 (ebook)

To the brilliant and hardworking animators. Your passion and talent have inspired so many.

CONTENTS

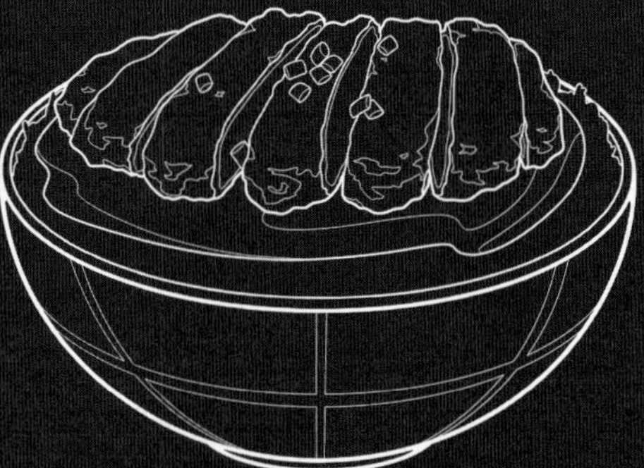

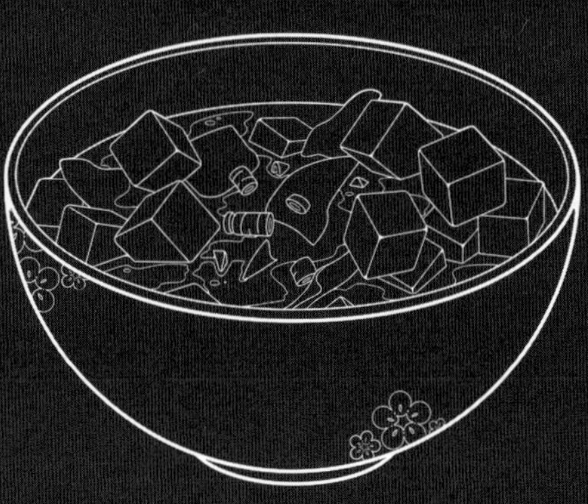

WHAT A SCRUMPTIOUS ABUNDANCE OF FOOD THERE IS IN ANIME!

The care that the creators and animators put into this facet of the art form is so impressive, and one of the aspects that sets Japanese animation apart from other animated media.

The food in anime can act as a window onto Japanese culture and history, and can bring even more meaning to the scene it's featured in. I was so intrigued by this that I wanted to explore it—and this book was developed from my perspective as an outsider looking in.

Even though I love the concept of food created specifically for a work of fiction (meaning that the food is unique to that work), the criterion that I set for this cookbook is that the food must have a real-world equivalent in order to explore my theme of learning more about Japan through the food found in anime.

The entries in this book came about in a couple of ways: seeing a dish in an anime, being intrigued, and then tracking it down in the real world, or the reverse—knowing of or happening upon a real-world food during research and then finding it in anime. Both methods were fun, as I enjoy matching things together (I spent too much time on this, perhaps; it was like a game). Delving into the cultural and historical aspects of the food and seeing how it's woven into the background or narrative of an anime is just so interesting to me.

To create the recipes for each entry, I researched different versions of the food to find the root of the recipe, referenced the anime (as well as the manga in some cases), and came up with a version that seemed accessible. Certain ingredients were a bit tricky to find, so that also shaped some of the recipes and, in some instances, guided the decision about whether to include the food in the book.

It's my hope that those who pick up this book, foodies and *otaku* alike (and the lovely people who are both), will enjoy the recipes and the stories behind them!

JAPANESE PANTRY

The following ingredients are helpful to have on hand when cooking with *Cook Anime*. All can be found in Japanese grocery stores or online.

Aburaage: Deep-fried tofu pouches, usually found in the refrigerated or freezer section.

Adzuki beans: The main ingredient in anko, a sweet red bean paste used in Japanese desserts.

Aonori: An edible green seaweed that is dried and powdered.

Beni-shoga: Ginger pickled in plum vinegar, which gives it a red hue.

Chuka soba noodles: Japanese for "thin Chinese noodles," this is the Japanese version of the wheat noodles used in ramen.

Doubanjiang: A chili paste made from fermented broad beans, also known as toban djan.

Enoki mushrooms: Called enokitake in Japanese, these long, thin white mushrooms are popular in soups, salads, and many other East Asian dishes.

Green tea: Japanese variations include karigane, kuchika, and sencha.

Joshinko: A non-glutinous rice flour made from milled short-grain rice.

Kabocha: A Japanese variety of winter squash with bumpy green skin (sometimes with stripes) on the outside and yellow-orange flesh on the inside.

Kakinotane: A preferred type of rice crackers.

Katakuriko: A fine potato starch used as a thickener.

Katsuobushi: Dried, fermented, and smoked fish flakes, also known as bonito.

Kewpie mayonnaise: Made with egg yolks instead of whole eggs, this mayo has a deeper yellow color and an umami flavor.

Kombu: An edible kelp, usually dried.

La-yu: A Japanese sesame oil made with hot chili peppers.

Matcha: Green tea leaves finely ground into a powder.

Mirin: A sweet Japanese rice wine similar to sake but with more sugar and lower alcohol content.

Miso paste: Available in white (shiso), red (aka), or black (douchi), this paste is made from fermented soybeans.

Mizuna: Japanese mustard greens. Celery leaves are an acceptable substitute.

Nagaimo: A root vegetable, often cooked like a potato.

Narutomaki: A type of kamaboko, this is a cured fish cake, used mainly as decoration.

Nori: An edible seaweed usually purchased dried; can also be found roasted.

Oroshi: Finely grated daikon.

Rice vinegar: Also known as rice wine vinegar and made from fermented rice. Seasoned rice vinegar has salt and sugar added and is used when making sushi rice. Apple cider vinegar is an acceptable substitute.

Satsumaimo: Japanese sweet potato.

Shichimi togarashi: A spicy dried chili pepper seasoning.

Shio kombu: Thin sheets of salted and sweet kombu.

Shirataki noodles: Made from konjac yam, these gelatinous noodles are super flavor-absorbent.

Shiratamako: A type of glutinous rice flour, also called sweet rice flour.

Shiso: An herb that's a member of the mint family, also known as perilla.

Umeboshi: Salted pickled plums.

Usukuchi: A light-colored soy sauce that is actually saltier in taste than the darker version, used only for cooking.

Wakame: An edible seaweed served in soups and salads, and often purchased dried.

Yamaimo: A Japanese golden yam, similar to a sweet potato.

ONE

MAIN DISHES

THE GREAT PASSAGE

SHIOZAKE

Salted Salmon Fillet

SERVES 2 Majime Mitsuya loves words and their myriad meanings but has difficulty expressing himself. A chance encounter lands him the job of his dreams: working on a new Japanese dictionary called *Daitokai* with a determined and tight-knit group. Majime puts all his passion and dedication into the endeavor over the years, finding love and courage along the way—sailing the vast ocean of words on the ship he's helping to build in order to bring people closer together through understanding. When the work stretches on and he needs a moment of rest and revitalization, he goes home to a warm meal of rice, miso soup, and shiozake prepared by someone he loves.

2 6-ounce salmon fillets, or 1 salmon steak cut in two, deboned, skin left on

1 tablespoon sake rice wine

2 teaspoons fine sea salt, or more to taste

1 Rinse the fillets under cold water and pat dry with paper towels. Coat the fillets in the sake and let sit for 5 minutes. Lightly pat the fillets with a paper towel again, then rub 1 teaspoon salt over each fillet. If you'd like a more intense salt flavor, add another half teaspoon of salt each, or to your taste. Generously wrap each fillet in paper towels and place them in a closed plastic or glass container. Place the container in the refrigerator overnight or for up to 2 days; the longer the time, the saltier the fish will be.

2 Preheat your oven to 400°F and line a baking sheet or oven-safe dish with lightly scrunched-up and re-flattened aluminum foil (scrunching the foil will help the salmon not stick to it). Unwrap the fillets and gently pat off any extra moisture with a fresh paper towel. Lay the fillets, skin side up, on the foil and bake on the middle rack for 20 minutes, or until the flesh is flaky and the skin is crispy.

FOOD FACTS Shiozake (sometimes referred to as shiojake) is a traditional breakfast item in Japan, often served alongside Miso Soup (page 56), Rice (page 52), Tamagoyaki (page 61), and pickle and vegetable side dishes. It's refreshing with a lemon wedge or a little mound of daikon oroshi (finely grated daikon radish). The salmon can also be flaked apart and used as an Onigiri filling (page 62), or as a topping for rice dishes such as a donburi or Chazuke (page 33).

Another common and less time-consuming way that salmon is prepared in Japan is to coat the salmon in sake and let it sit for 5 minutes (as in this recipe), and then, after patting the fish dry with a paper towel, lightly salt the fillets and let them sit for only 5 minutes. Pat off the resulting moisture with another paper towel. Place the fish on an oiled rack over a tray of water and broil, skin side up, for 10 minutes, then flip and cook for another 5 minutes. Because this way is quicker, the salt doesn't permeate the fish as much.

ANIME FACTS "Daitokai" translates to "the great passage." "Passage" could mean a segment of writing, a reference to traveling, a place to travel through, or even the sliding by of time. All of these are applicable to the story. *The Great Passage* anime is an adaptation of the book *Fune wo amu* by Shion Miura, published in 2011. The title translates to "knitting the boat," which is very apt. The award-winning book was first adapted into a live-action film (which also won many awards) and eventually the anime series *The Great Passage*. Miura is also the author of *Kaze ga Tsuyoku Fuiteiru*, which was adapted into a live-action film and the inspiring anime series *Run with the Wind*.

THIS FOOD ALSO APPEARS IN . . .

- *Weathering with You*
- *Someone's Gaze*
- *Log Horizon*
- *How I Miss You*
- *Tokyo Ghoul: Root A*
- *Witchy PreCure!*
- *Wakakozake*
- *Hanasaku Iroha: Blossoms for Tomorrow*
- *AKB0048*
- *Natsume's Book of Friends*
- *Monthly Girls' Nozaki-Kun*
- *Kuromukuro*
- *Keijo!!!!!!!!*
- *Space Brothers*
- *Age 12*
- *The Helpful Fox Senko-san*

DEMON SLAYER: KIMETSU NO YAIBA

TEMPURA

Deep-Fried, Batter-Dipped Vegetables and Shrimp

SERVES 2 After fighting a powerful demon (and each other), Tanjiro, Zenitsu, and Inosuke are guided to a house with a wisteria family crest where their wounds are treated, their clothes are washed and mended, and their stomachs are filled with delicious food. The wild Inosuke in particular gobbles up the homemade tempura and gets the warm fuzzies when the elderly lady of the house kindly offers to make him more.

FOR THE TEMPURA BATTER

- **1 large egg, chilled**
- **1 cup ice water (strain ice cubes before using)**
- **1 cup flour, chilled and sifted three times**

HISA'S TEMPURA INGREDIENTS

- **6 extra-large shrimp, prepared as for Ebi Furai (page 18)**
- **6 green beans, stem ends discarded**
- **⅓ kabocha squash (also known as winter squash), skin left on, sliced ¼ inch thick**
- **½ lotus root, peeled and sliced ¼ inch thick**
- **1 Japanese sweet potato (satsumaimo), skin left on, sliced ¼ inch thick**
- **4 shiso leaves (also called perilla leaves)**
- **¼ cup cornstarch or potato starch**
- **Vegetable or canola oil, for frying**
- **2 tablespoons oroshi (finely grated daikon radish)**

FOR THE TENTSUYU DIPPING SAUCE

- **½ cup Dashi Stock (page 56)**
- **2 tablespoons soy sauce**
- **2 tablespoons mirin**
- **1 teaspoon sugar**

1 Prepare the shrimp and vegetables, pat with paper towels to get rid of moisture, and toss with the starch. In a heavy-bottomed pot, bring 1½ to 2 inches of oil to 365°F. (Don't make the batter until the oil is steadily holding its temperature. Until then, keep the batter ingredients cold.) Once the oil is at 365°F, use chopsticks to whisk the egg lightly with the ice water. Add the flour and stir the mixture in a figure-eight motion until just combined. Don't worry about lumps—do not overmix.

2 Dip the prepared shrimp in the batter and lay them in the oil, making sure not to crowd the pot. Cook for 1 to 2 minutes, using chopsticks or tongs to flip so all sides get crispy. Lay the cooked shrimp on a wire rack with paper towels or foil underneath. Skim out any batter bits floating in the oil and place on paper towels (see Food Facts below). Coat the remaining ingredients with batter, again making sure not to crowd the pot, and cook until crispy.

3 Make the tentsuyu dipping sauce: Combine all of the ingredients in a small pot over medium-low heat and cook until the sugar is dissolved. Serve warm alongside freshly made tempura and oroshi, which is often mixed into the sauce.

FOOD FACTS Other common tempura ingredients include mushrooms, broccoli, onions, asparagus, eggplant, and zucchini. Try out different foods, but make sure to avoid those that have a lot of moisture.

To make tempura fritters called kakiage, like Bulma treats Whis to in *Dragon Ball Super*, simply julienne your ingredients, toss lightly with starch, and coat in tempura batter. Scoop ⅓ cup of the mixture into the 365°F oil and quickly spread out with chopsticks to make a thin patty shape. Cook on both sides until crispy, 2 to 3 minutes. This is also a good way to use up extra tempura batter. Common ingredients for kakiage include green beans, onion, small asparagus, carrot, small shrimp, burdock root, sweet potato, and shiso leaves. You can even try using Kinpira Gobo (page 71). Place the kakiage on a bowl of rice for kakiage don!

Make sure not to throw away those tempura bits! The little fried bits of batter are called tenkasu (or sometimes agedama) and are used in Okonomiyaki (page 89), Takoyaki (page 87), and for Udon (page 26), among other things. As you're frying your tempura, skim out the tenkasu and spread them out on a plate lined with paper towels. You can also make tenkasu with leftover tempura batter by using chopsticks to drizzle the batter into the oil. Let cook until golden, 20 to 30 seconds, then skim them off and spread them out on paper towels to cool. Store for up to a week in an airtight container in the refrigerator. You can sometimes find tenkasu in Asian grocery stores, but if you're making tempura, why not save the bits? Tenkasu means "heavenly waste," after all.

CULTURE FACTS The name "tempura" comes from the Latin word *tempora*. In the 1500s, many Portuguese Catholic missionaries resided in Japan, and during the *quatuor anni tempora*, or four seasons of fasting (also known as Quatuor Tempora and Ember Days), when eating red meat was forbidden, they would often eat batter-dipped seafood and vegetables. Battered and fried foods were not part of the Japanese diet before this, but the practice grew in popularity over time and was adapted to Japanese tastes. Tempura is now seen as a quintessential Japanese dish.

THIS FOOD ALSO APPEARS IN . . .

- *Takunomi*
- *Nora, Princess, and Stray Cat*
- *Yamada-Kun and the Seven Witches*
- *Hanasaku Iroha: Blossoms for Tomorrow*
- *Fancy Lala*
- *THE IDOLM@STER*
- *K-On!*
- *The Quintessential Quintuplets*
- *Dragon Ball Super*
- *Bunny Drop*
- *Nichijou—My Ordinary Life*
- *Fate/stay night*
- *Sakura Quest*

PENGUINDRUM

KARE

Meat and Vegetables in Sauce with Rice

SERVES 4 TO 6 Entangled in fate and unfortunate pasts, the Takakura siblings Kanba, Shoma, and Himari navigate a world of colliding destinies, desperate passions, an uncaring and cruel society, righteous terrorism gone awry, and . . . magical penguins. Himari's fragile life is prolonged by an envoy from a special penguin who tasks Kanba and Shoma with finding the mysterious "penguindrum." As they search, they reveal chains linking their lives with those of certain others such as Ringo Oginome, who possesses an incredible diary, desires to live out her dead sister's unfinished life, and observes Curry Day, a special family day, each month. Remember, curry tastes like happiness when eaten with people you love.

- **½ pound boneless, skinless chicken thigh or pork, cut into bite-size pieces**
- **½ sweet apple (such as Gala), peeled, cored, and finely grated**
- **1 tablespoon honey**
- **1 tablespoon vegetable or canola oil**
- **1 large onion, cut into bite-size pieces**
- **1 large potato, peeled, cut into bite-size pieces**
- **2 large carrots, peeled, cut into bite-size pieces**
- **2 cups chicken or vegetable broth (or substitute 2 cups water)**
- **1 tablespoon soy sauce**
- **1 tablespoon mirin**
- **6 blocks Curry Roux (recipe follows)**
- **1 to 2 tablespoons apple preserves, jam, or jelly**
- **Salt and freshly ground black pepper**
- **6 cups cooked Rice (page 52)**

1 In a medium bowl, toss together the chicken or pork, grated apple, and honey; cover with plastic wrap and let marinate for 20 minutes in the refrigerator. Bring back to room temperature for 10 minutes before using.

2 Heat the oil in a large, wide pot over medium heat, then add the onions and sauté until tender, about 10 minutes. Stir in the marinated meat mixture and cook until no longer pink, about 5 minutes. Stir in the potatoes and carrots, then add in the broth, 1 cup water, the soy sauce, and mirin. Simmer, uncovered, for 15 minutes.

3 Add in the Curry Roux blocks and stir until dissolved and the curry has thickened, 10 to 15 minutes more. Remove from the heat and stir in the apple preserves, according to your taste for sweetness. Season with salt and pepper, if needed. Serve with the cooked white rice—rice on one side of the dish and curry on the other.

FOOD FACTS In *Penguindrum*, we learn about Ringo's variation on traditional Japanese curry, made to suit Tabuki's taste. She uses either pork or chicken as the meat and marinates it with grated apple, reduces the amount of carrots and adds extra potato to compensate, and adds apple jam, honey, and extra cumin. You can make the curry to suit your tastes by omitting the meat if you'd like, adding different vegetables, or adding chili powder to the roux along with the other spices for more heat. By the way, did you know that *ringo* means "apple" in Japanese?

ANIME FACTS There are many references and allusions in *Penguindrum*, but one that permeates the whole series is a reference to Kenji Miyazawa's 1930s novel *Night on the Galactic Railroad* and its 1985 anime adaptation. There are the colors of blue and red, the tale of the self-sacrificing scorpion, and, in both the first and last episodes of *Penguindrum*, two boys are talking about the meaningful motif of apples in Miyazawa's story.

Curry is often shown in anime during camping or training scenes or when the characters stay overnight at the beach because it is easy to put together, especially if you use premade Curry Roux.

Japanese curry differs from Indian and Thai curry in that it is typically not as spicy, and is sweeter. Curry served with rice is known as *kare raisu* in Japan, but curry is also used in many other dishes, such as curry udon found in *Inu x Boku SS*, curry ramen, katsu curry as seen in *Devilman Crybaby*, and hambagu curry (often with cheese!). You could even put curry in a bread bowl like in *Comet Lucifer*. You might remember the prize-winning curry bread or kare pan that Sebastian Michaelis makes in *Black Butler* that includes chocolate. Curry with dark chocolate added is actually not uncommon in Japan, and is referred to as *kuro kare* or "black curry." Sometimes, to get a signature black color, squid ink is added (*Squid Girl*, anyone?).

Curry bread is also what started the rivalry between Ranma and Ryoga in *Ranma ½*.

THIS FOOD ALSO APPEARS IN . . .

- *Samurai Flamenco*
- *Air*
- *Run with the Wind*
- *Kanon*
- *Suite PreCure*
- *Saint Seiya Omega*
- *Dino Girl Gauko*
- *Log Horizon*
- *Happy Sugar Life*
- *My Hero Academia*
- *Etotama*
- *Amanchu!*
- *Genshiken*
- *Sweetness & Lightning*
- *Parasyte -the maxim-*
- *Shuffle!*
- *Masamune-kun's Revenge*
- *Silver Spoon*

CURRY ROUX BLOCKS

- **1/3 cup unsalted butter, cubed**
- **1/3 cup plus 2 tablespoons all-purpose flour**
- **3 tablespoons curry powder**
- **2 tablespoons ground cumin**
- **1 teaspoon allspice**
- **1/2 teaspoon garlic salt**
- **1/2 teaspoon onion powder**
- **1/8 teaspoon ground ginger**

1 In a medium pot over medium-low heat, melt the butter. Add the flour and stir to create a smooth consistency. Continue to stir until the mixture turns caramel in color. Add the curry powder, cumin, allspice, garlic salt, onion powder, and ginger and stir to combine. Cook for another 30 seconds, then remove from the heat.

2 Let the curry roux cool down for a few minutes, stirring occasionally as it begins to solidify. Spoon the mixture onto a large sheet of plastic wrap, and fold the sides up and over to cover the roux. Pat the wrapped roux into a square about 1/2 inch thick and place in the refrigerator to solidify completely. When you'd like to use the roux, unwrap it and cut it into 6 equal blocks.

NATSUME'S BOOK OF FRIENDS

EBI FURAI

Deep-Fried Breaded Shrimp

SERVES 2 Having inherited the ability to interact with yokai (folklore spirits or demons) from his mysterious grandmother, Takashi Natsume has had a difficult life trying to balance the human world and the supernatural. After being taken in by distant but kindly relatives, Natsume discovers his grandmother's "Book of Friends," filled with the names of yokai she met long ago. He also unwittingly releases a powerful yokai named Madara, who decides to stick with Natsume in order to one day obtain the Book of Friends. Madara assumes the form of a chubby, mochi-like cat named Nyanko-sensei who loves to drink sake and eat manju and ebi furai—and pretty much anything else. Like Nyanko-sensei, do you think ebi furai tails look like hearts?

- **10 raw jumbo or extra-large shrimp, peeled and deveined with tail on**
- **1 tablespoon cornstarch**
- **1 tablespoon sake**
- **½ cup all-purpose flour**
- **1 large egg**
- **1 cup panko bread crumbs**
- **Vegetable or canola oil, for frying**
- **Salt and freshly ground black pepper**

FOR THE TARTAR SAUCE

- **1 hard-boiled egg, shelled and minced**
- **1 heaping tablespoon Kewpie mayonnaise**
- **1 tablespoon minced onion**
- **1 tablespoon minced dill pickle**
- **1 to 2 teaspoons minced fresh flat-leaf parsley**
- **1 teaspoon lemon juice**
- **Salt and freshly ground black pepper**

1 Snip the shrimps' tail fins into a V and remove the small shell piece at the center base of the tail. Cut 5 to 6 slits across the stomach of the shrimp, making sure not to go all the way through, then bend the shrimp backwards, snapping many of the fibers. This will help the shrimp stay relatively straight when fried. Toss the shrimp in the cornstarch, then rinse and pat with paper towels. Put the shrimp in a bowl, toss with the sake, and let sit for about 10 minutes.

2 Put the flour in a medium bowl. In another medium bowl, beat the egg well. Put the panko in a third medium bowl. Line these up near your deep fryer or stovetop in the order listed. In a deep, heavy-bottomed pot, heat at least 2 inches of oil to 350°F. Pat the shrimp with paper towels, then sprinkle lightly with salt and pepper. Working one at a time, dredge the shrimp in flour, then dip in egg. Repeat dredging in flour and egg a second time, then coat in panko, squeezing the shrimp gently in your fist to compact the crumb coating. Lay the prepared shrimp on a plate or paper towel until ready to fry. Repeat this coating process with the remaining shrimp.

3 Fry 3 to 4 shrimp at a time, depending on the size of your pot—you don't want to overcrowd. Watch the temperature, keeping the oil at 350°F. Cook the shrimp for 2 minutes per side, until golden brown; using tongs is very helpful for moving the shrimp around. Remove the cooked shrimp to a paper towel–covered baking sheet or plate, or a wire cooling rack set over a baking sheet. Repeat the frying process with all of the shrimp.

4 Make the tartar sauce: Simply stir together all of the ingredients in a small bowl, keeping the sauce relatively chunky, and serve with the fried shrimp.

FOOD FACTS Ebi furai can be served as a main course, but it is a very common addition to bento (page 78), as seen in *THE IDOLM@STER*, *Sailor Moon R*, and many other anime. You can also roll ebi furai in Sushi Rice (page 52) and nori seaweed for ebi maki sushi!

Ebi furai and shrimp tempura are sometimes mixed up when seen in anime. While ebi furai is coated in panko, shrimp tempura is dipped in a flour batter (see page 15). Aji furai, which is also breaded in panko, is another dish sometimes confused with ebi furai when seen in anime, but it's made with tail-on horse mackerel fillets instead of shrimp or prawns. You can see aji furai in *Aikatsu!* and *From Up on Poppy Hill*.

THIS FOOD ALSO APPEARS IN . . .

- *Ninjaboy Rantaro*
- *THE IDOLM@STER*
- *Sailor Moon R*
- *The Melancholy of Haruhi Suzumiya*
- *Squid Girl*
- *Restaurant to Another World*
- *Tari Tari*
- *Urahara*
- *Minori Scramble!*
- *A Lull in the Sea*
- *Little Busters!*
- *Blue Spring Ride*
- *Log Horizon*

NARUTO

MISO CHASHU RAMEN

Noodle Soup with Braised Pork and Miso Broth

SERVES 2 An outcast in his village because of the destructive power sealed inside of him and the devastating history attached to it, young Naruto Uzumaki has one solace: the warm noodle soup at Ichiraku Ramen—with extra chashu pork, of course.

1 tablespoon sesame oil
¼ large onion, minced
1-inch piece fresh ginger, peeled and minced
2 teaspoons minced garlic
¼ pound ground pork
3 tablespoons miso paste, shiro (white) or aka (red), or a mixture of the two
2 cups chicken stock
1 cup Dashi Stock (page 56)
2 tablespoons mirin
3 green onions, dark green parts and roots discarded, plus 1 extra green onion, chopped, for garnish
Salt and white pepper, to taste
La-yu chili oil (optional)
6 ounces ramen or chuka soba noodles, fresh-packed or dried
10 to 14 slices Chashu Pork (recipe follows)
Menma (recipe follows)
2 Ajitsuke Tamago (recipe follows)
4 narutomaki kamabuko fishcake slices
6 roasted nori sheets

1 Heat the sesame oil in a large pot over medium-low heat and add the onion, ginger, and garlic. Cook until just tender and fragrant, about 10 minutes. Add the ground pork, breaking up the meat with a wooden spoon. Cook until the meat is no longer pink, about 5 minutes, and then stir in the miso paste until evenly distributed. Pour in the chicken stock, dashi stock, and mirin. Add the green onion and increase the heat to medium. Bring to a simmer, then reduce the heat to medium-low. Simmer for 10 minutes, skimming off the foam as needed.

2 Strain the soup through a fine-mesh strainer into a large pitcher or pot, reserving the solids for rice or ramen toppings if desired. Season with salt and white pepper, and the la-yu oil, if using.

3 Bring a large pot of water to boil and stir in the noodles. Cook according to package directions, about 3 minutes, until the noodles are just tender and cooked all the way through. Drain but don't rinse and divide into 2 serving bowls. Spoon broth over the noodles, then top each with 5 to 7 overlapping slices of chashu, menma, chopped green onion, 2 slices of narutomaki, 1 ramen egg cut in half, and 3 sheets of nori.

CHASHU PORK

1 cup sake rice wine

1 cup soy sauce

½ cup packed dark brown sugar

3 green onions and/or 1 leek, dark green parts and roots discarded, cut into 2-inch segments

2-inch piece fresh ginger, unpeeled, sliced very thinly

1 to 1½ pounds pork belly, skin removed

1 tablespoon vegetable oil

1 In a large, deep pot over high heat, combine 2 cups of water with the sake, soy sauce, sugar, green onions or leek, and ginger. Roll the pork belly tightly into a log and secure very snuggly with baker's twine in at least 5 equally spaced spots. Place a large skillet over high heat and add the oil. Once the pan is very hot, sear the rolled meat well on all sides, 2 to 3 minutes per side. Transfer the meat to the deep pot and stir to coat with the marinade. Bring the marinade to a boil, skim off any foam, then reduce the heat to medium-low. Cover the pot and cook for 2 hours, rotating the meat every so often in the marinade and skimming foam as needed.

2 Remove the pot from the heat and let the meat cool in the marinade. Remove the meat from the pot and place in a sturdy zip-top bag. Strain and reserve the marinating liquid, pouring enough into the bag with the meat to cover. Refrigerate overnight. The leftover marinade can be used to make the Menma and Ajitsuke Tamago ramen toppings (recipes follow), which also marinate overnight.

3 The next day, preheat your oven to broil and line a baking sheet with aluminum foil or parchment paper. Remove the meat from the bag and discard any solidified fat bits. Cut the strings and slice the meat into ¼-inch-thick slices. Place the slices on the baking sheet and broil for 2 to 3 minutes, just until the meat crisps up. Serve on top of the ramen—Naruto often gets 5 to 7 slices on his.

NOTES Chashu pork is the Japanese adaptation of Cantonese char siu roasted pork, and differs in seasonings, preparation, and cooking. Char siu uses long strips of pork and is roasted, whereas chashu uses rolled pork and is slow braised.

Chashu is not only great on ramen but also as a donburi, simply placed atop a bowl of rice. The other marinated ingredients are flavorful additions.

To make chashu chicken instead of pork, use 1 pound boneless chicken thighs (skin on is fine). Lay the chicken out, pieces overlapping one another, flaying as needed to make it flat, then roll up and tie just like the pork. Continue with the same steps, but only simmer in the marinade for 30 minutes, making sure the internal temperature of the chicken is 165°F. No need to broil just before serving.

MENMA

1 cup plain bamboo shoot strips (if using dried, rehydrate in cold water for 3 hours)

½ cup Chashu marinade (see recipe above)

½ cup mirin

1 cup Dashi Stock (page 56)

1 In a medium pot over medium heat, combine all of the ingredients and bring to a boil. Cover, reduce the heat to low, and simmer for 30 minutes, until the bamboo is softened.

2 Remove from the heat and let the bamboo cool in the liquid. Pour everything into a freezer bag or plastic container and marinate in the refrigerator overnight. Strain when ready to use.

NOTE Menma, marinated sliced bamboo, is a common ramen topping, and is also the name of Naruto's alternate universe counterpart in *Road to Ninja: Naruto the Movie*.

AJITSUKE TAMAGO

2 large eggs

1/2 cup Chashu marinade (see recipe above)

1 Fill a medium pot with enough water to cover the eggs. (Do not put the eggs in the pot at this time.) Bring the water to a boil, then reduce to medium heat. Lower the eggs into the water and gently roll them around for 2 minutes, then let them cook for exactly 4 more minutes. While the eggs are cooking, prepare an ice bath by filling a medium bowl with enough cold water to cover the eggs and several ice cubes. Once the eggs are cooked, quickly remove them from the water and place them in the ice bath to cool.

2 Once cool, gently tap and roll the eggs on the countertop to crack the shells all over. Carefully peel away the shell, then place the eggs in a freezer bag. Pour the marinade over the eggs and seal the bag. Marinate in the refrigerator overnight. When ready to serve, remove the eggs from the liquid and carefully slice in half lengthwise; the whites will be solid and the yolks will be runny.

NOTES If you'd like to make Ajitsuke Tamago independent from Chashu and its marinade, combine 1/4 cup soy sauce, 1/4 cup mirin, and 1 teaspoon of honey or brown sugar for the egg marinade instead.

Ajitsuke tamago are sometimes called ajitama (seasoned eggs) or simply ramen eggs, and are characterized by their solid whites and runny yolks. For jammy centers, cook the eggs for 7 minutes, and for hard-boiled, cook for 9 minutes.

FOOD FACTS The narutomaki kamabuko fish cake gets its name and design inspiration from the whirlpools of the Naruto Strait in Hyogo, Japan. Thus, the character Naruto's first name is an allusion not only to the ramen topping but also to the powerfully swirling waters. Likewise, Naruto's clan name, Uzumaki, also means "whirlpool." So it's a double whirlpool whammy!

CULTURE FACTS Ichiraku Ramen, Naruto's favorite ramen shop in the series, exists in real life in Fukuoka, Japan. The word *ichiraku* conveys the meaning of "number one comfort" or "hobby." What a perfect idea, as good ramen is both comforting and makes you want to come back for more!

ANIME FACTS While Ichiraku Ramen might be Naruto's favorite eating place, Hinata Hyuga holds its ramen-eating-contest record of forty-six bowls. Naruto took Hinata to Ichiraku on their first date, and it became her favorite place, too.

THIS FOOD ALSO APPEARS IN . . .

- *Case Closed*
- *Dragon Ball Super*
- *Space Dandy*
- *Kamen Rider W*
- *Ms. Koizumi Loves Ramen Noodles*
- *Ramen Fighter Miki*
- *Urusei Yatsura*
- *Amagami SS*
- *THE IDOLM@STER*
- *Symphogear*

NIKUJAGA

Stewed Meat and Potatoes

SERVES 2 In an alternate Tokyo, ghouls live secretly in society and survive on the flesh of humans. If they ingest anything else—aside from coffee—their body will violently reject it. Touka Kirishima keeps the fact that she's a ghoul hidden from her human best friend, Yoriko, whose companionship and normalcy Touka holds very dear. However, when Touka becomes sick and Yoriko drops off a pot of homemade nikujaga to help her feel better, Touka forces herself to eat it so as not to let the care and good intentions of her friend go to waste.

- **1 large potato, peeled**
- **½ (8-ounce) package shirataki noodles, drained**
- **1 cup Dashi Stock (page 56)**
- **2 tablespoons soy sauce**
- **2 tablespoons sake**
- **2 tablespoons mirin**
- **1½ teaspoons sugar**
- **½ large onion, cut into bite-size wedges**
- **1 tablespoon vegetable or canola oil**
- **¼ pound very thinly sliced beef short rib or pork belly, cut into 2-inch-long pieces**
- **1 large carrot, peeled and cut into bite-size pieces**
- **8 green beans, halved, ends discarded**
- **1 tablespoon fresh or frozen peas**

1 Cut the potato into rounded bite-size pieces; this will prevent them from falling apart when cooking. Place the potato pieces in cold water and set aside until needed. Rinse the shirataki noodles under very hot water, drain, and cut in half.

2 In a glass measuring cup or pitcher, combine the dashi stock, soy sauce, sake, mirin, and sugar and whisk until the sugar is dissolved. In a large pot over medium heat, sauté the onion wedges in the oil until tender, about 12 minutes. Add the meat and cook just until no longer pink, about 4 minutes. Add the carrot, potato, and noodles, then pour in the liquid mixture. Bring to a simmer over medium heat, skimming off any foam as needed, then reduce the heat to medium-low. Do not stir. Fold a sheet of aluminum foil into a disc that can fit into the pot to rest directly on top of the ingredients. Poke a few holes in the disc and place it in the pot. Simmer for 20 minutes, or until the carrots are tender. Turn off the heat and let cool on the stove for 30 minutes.

3 In a small pot of boiling water, blanch the green beans for 30 seconds. Add the peas, blanch for another 30 seconds, then drain. Remove the foil disc from the pot and gently fold in the beans and peas.

NOTES Nikujaga is a portmanteau of niku for "meat" and jaga from jagaimo for "potato." It's a type of nimono, or "simmered dish." Thin-sliced beef is often used, but thin-sliced pork can be used as well. In *Tokyo Ghoul*, Yoriko used green beans and peas for the greens in her nikujaga, but snow peas are also common, and you could use broccoli, too. Shirataki noodles (shirataki meaning "white waterfall") are made from the konjac yam and are a common ingredient in nikujaga for texture and flavor absorption, but you can leave them out if you'd like. The foil disk is a makeshift otoshibutta, or drop lid, which keeps the ingredients submerged while cooking.

FOOD FACTS Nikujaga is a Japanese dish fondly referred to as ofukuro no aji or "mother's taste." This is usually said when someone is nostalgic for the flavor of their mother's cooking. Other ofukuro no aji foods are Miso Soup (page 56), kabocha-ni simmered kabocha pumpkin (see below); saba no misoni, or simmered mackerel; and shogayaki, or ginger pork.

To make kabocha nimono (or kabocha-ni), cut half of a kabocha into 2-inch bite-size pieces, discarding the seeds and strings but keeping on the green skin. Place the pieces in a large, wide pot, as much in a single layer as possible, and pour in the same cooking liquid as for nikujaga, but only enough to just cover the kabocha. Lay the foil drop lid on top and simmer until the kabocha is tender, about 20 minutes, adding more broth if it evaporates before the kabocha is done. Turn off the heat, cover, and let sit for another 20 minutes. You can find this dish in *Shirobako, The Garden of Words*, and *Log Horizon*, and in many other anime as both a side dish and in bento.

CULTURE FACTS The conception of Nikujaga in the late 1800s is attributed to Admiral Togo of the Japanese Imperial Navy, who trained for many years in England and was inspired by the meat-and-potato stew served to British soldiers. Togo wanted something hearty and filling, full of protein and carbohydrates, for his own men, and thus this fusion dish was created. Nikujaga is an example of "yoshoku" food, or food that is influenced by cultures outside of Japan's. The dish has gone on to become a well-loved and popular Japanese home meal.

Did you know that Nikujaga is Domo's favorite food? Domo-kun is the furry monster mascot of Japan's national broadcasting organization Nippon Hyoso Kyokai, more commonly known as NHK.

THIS FOOD ALSO APPEARS IN . . .

- *Take My Brother Away*
- *Brynhildr in the Darkness*
- *Death Parade*
- *My Love Story!!*
- *Fate/stay night: Unlimited Blade Works*
- *Penguindrum*
- *Gintama*
- *THE IDOLM@STER*
- *When Supernatural Battles Became Commonplace*
- *Monthly Girls' Nozaki-Kun*
- *Nanana's Buried Treasure*

POCO'S UDON WORLD

UDON

Thick Wheat Flour Noodles

SERVES 2 After his father's death, Souta Tawara visits his hometown in Kanagawa to get things in order to sell the family home and udon restaurant. While checking on the old shop and finding a mysterious child—with fluffy ears and a tail—sleeping in an old flour barrel, Souta's life changes drastically, and he's no longer sure if he wants to close the door on his past.

1 teaspoon salt
⅓ cup hot water
1 cup all-purpose flour
Cornstarch, for dusting

MENTSUYU NOODLE BROTH

1 cup Dashi Stock (page 56)
3 tablespoons soy sauce
3 tablespoons mirin
½ teaspoon sugar

1 Combine the salt with the hot water and let it sit for several minutes to dissolve. Sift the flour into a large bowl and pour the salt water in gradually, kneading the mixture with your hands to create a cohesive dough.

2 Form the dough into a ball and place it in the center of a plastic gallon freezer bag, not sealed, then place that bag inside another gallon freezer bag in the opposite direction, also not sealed. Lay the bags on an uncarpeted floor and knead the dough with your socked or bare feet. Don't stomp, but shift your weight back and forth to work the surface of the dough ("one, two, udon, udon"). Do this for 4 minutes, then reshape the dough into a ball and knead again with your feet for another 4 minutes. Let the dough rest on the counter, still in the plastic bags, for 30 minutes. Repeat the kneading process. Afterward, remove the dough from the bags, shape it back into a ball, and return it to the bags. Seal the bags and let the dough rest on the counter for 3 hours.

3 Lightly dust a flat work surface with cornstarch. Knead the dough in the bags with your feet for a few seconds just to get it loosened up again, then remove the dough and lay it on your work surface. Dust the dough lightly with cornstarch and roll into a rectangle of ⅛ inch thickness. Lightly dust both sides of the dough with more cornstarch and fold the dough into thirds lengthwise, like a brochure. Using a large, sharp knife, slice the folded dough into ⅛-inch strips. Dust them a bit more with cornstarch and stretch them gently in any places that might be thicker or wider than others. Cover the noodles with a sheet of plastic.

4 In a large pot, bring 6 cups of water to a boil. Gently shake off any excess cornstarch from the noodles, then lower them into the boiling water. Cook for 12 minutes or until cooked through, stirring often so the noodles don't stick together, especially in the beginning. While the noodles are cooking, fill a large bowl halfway with cold water and add several ice cubes to create an ice bath. Strain the noodles, then dunk them in the ice bath for 30 seconds.

5 While the noodles are cooking, make the mentsuyu broth: In a small pot over medium heat, combine the dashi, soy sauce, mirin, and sugar. Bring to a steady simmer and cook for 5 minutes. Divide the noodles into 2 serving bowls. Pour the broth over the udon noodles and garnish as desired.

NOTE If you'd like to make Udon with an egg yolk on top, pasteurized eggs are recommended. If you can't find any in the store, you can make your own. Place an egg in a medium pot, cover with water, and, using a digital or candy thermometer, bring the temperature to a steady 140°F for 3 minutes. If the temperature starts to rise, adjust the heat or pour in a bit more water to bring it down. Rinse the egg under cold water and then use as directed.

FOOD FACTS Mentsuyu, which means "broth for noodles," can come in a concentrated form or a soup form, which is the one in this recipe. The concentrated version doesn't contain dashi stock as an ingredient; rather, the kombu and katsuobushi used in dashi are directly cooked with soy sauce and mirin and then strained out before using. The soup version of mentsuyu uses a combination of dashi stock with a premade, concentrated mixture called "kaeshi," which contains soy sauce, mirin, and sugar. Mentsuyu is made with varying measurements of ingredients all over Japan to suit individual tastes, so adjust the amounts in this recipe to your taste to get the mentsuyu that's right for you!

CULTURE FACTS Did you know that tanuki really exist? They're often taken for raccoons by those living outside of Japan, but, though their markings resemble those of raccoons, tanuki are actually a species in the canid family called raccoon dogs. In folklore, tanuki are regarded as yokai (supernatural beings) that can shape-shift and sometimes play tricks on humans.

THIS FOOD ALSO APPEARS IN . . .

- *Whisper of the Heart*
- *Space Brothers*
- *Demon Slayer: Kimetsu no Yaiba*
- *K-On!*
- *Atom: the Beginning*
- *Inu x Boku SS*
- *Wolf Girl & Black Prince*
- *Tamako Market*
- *Harukana Receive*
- *Touken Ranbu: Hanamaru*
- *Bunny Drop*
- *The Quintessential Quintuplets*

FOOD WARS!

MAPO TOFU

Tofu in Meat Sauce

SERVES 2 Spicy and delicious at the same time, mapo tofu can be served on its own or alongside cooked rice.

1 block (12.3 ounces) silken tofu

2 green onions, roots discarded

1 tablespoon vegetable or canola oil

1 tablespoon minced garlic

2 teaspoons minced ginger

½ pound ground pork, or a combination of ground pork and ground beef

2 to 3 tablespoons doubanjiang (broad bean chili paste, also called toban djan)

1 tablespoon douchi black soy bean paste or red miso paste

1 tablespoon oyster sauce

2 teaspoons Chinese red chili powder

¼ teaspoon sugar

2 tablespoons sake

1 tablespoon mirin

1 teaspoon soy sauce

¾ cup chicken stock

2 teaspoons cornstarch

1 Gently wrap the block of tofu in 3 layers of paper towels and place it between 2 cutting boards or baking sheets for 20 to 30 minutes. Carefully cut the tofu block into ½- to ¾-inch cubes. Bring a medium pot half-filled with water and a pinch of salt to a boil over medium-high heat. Once boiling, add the tofu cubes and cook for 2 minutes. Drain and set the tofu aside in the strainer until needed.

2 Mince the white part of the green onions and save the green parts for later. In a large pan over medium-low heat, add the oil, garlic, ginger, and the white parts of the green onions and cook until fragrant. Add the ground meat and break it into tiny pieces, cooking until no longer pink, about 3 minutes. Stir in the doubanjiang, black bean paste or miso, oyster sauce, chili powder, and sugar until evenly combined. Pour in the sake, mirin, soy sauce, and chicken stock. Cover the pan, increase the heat to medium, and let simmer for 5 minutes.

3 Completely dissolve the cornstarch in 1 tablespoon of water, then stir the mixture into the pan until well combined. Bring the mixture back up to a bubbling simmer.

4 Lightly fold the tofu cubes into the meat sauce, doing your best not to break them. Cover the pan, reduce the heat to medium-low, and simmer for another 5 minutes. Chop the green parts of the green onions and sprinkle on top of the mapo tofu when serving.

NOTE Japanese-style mapo tofu is not as spicy as the original Sichuan version, but if you'd like to give it the high heat and beautiful color that we see in *Food Wars!* and other anime like *Angel Beats!*, toast 1 to 2 teaspoons of Sichuan peppercorns in the pan before adding anything else, then grind them into a powder and set aside. Instead of using only 2 teaspoons of the bright red Chinese chili powder to the meat, add up to 1 tablespoon or more to suit your tastes. Fold in ¼ to ½ teaspoon of the freshly ground peppercorns to the mapo tofu at the very end.

FOOD FACTS Mapo tofu is an example of chuka ryori, meaning "Chinese food," sometimes simply called chuka. Chuka denotes dishes originating in China that have been adapted to Japanese styles and tastes. Other chuka food examples are Ramen (page 21), Chashu (page 22), Chinjao Rosu (page 43), Karaage (page 66), Nikuman (page 94), and Gyoza (page 68).

Mapo tofu, sometimes called mabo dofu, is a portmanteau of *má-zi*, meaning "pockmarks," and *popo*, meaning "grandmother." Apparently dear Mrs. Chen, the creator of this tasty dish at her little eatery in 1862 Chengdu, Sichuan, China, was an elderly lady with a pockmarked face. Let's hope it was an endearing name, as people loved her tofu dish so much that it went on to become popular around the world.

THIS FOOD ALSO APPEARS IN . . .

- *Angel Beats!*
- *Haikyuu!!: vs. Akaten*
- *Log Horizon*
- *Fate/stay night: Heaven's Feel*
- *Tales of Zestiria: Dawn of the Shepherd*
- *Sound! Euphonium*
- *Stars Align*
- *True Cooking Master Boy*

OURAN HIGH SCHOOL HOST CLUB

NABE

Hot Pot Meal

SERVES 4 TO 6 On a scholarship to the elite Ouran Academy, commoner Haruhi Fujioka unwittingly becomes a member of the school's host club after breaking an extremely expensive vase and being mistaken for a boy. The host club is run by six rich, handsome, and eccentric young men who entertain the female students of the school with tea, flattery, and cakes; much to their surprise, Haruhi is an exceptional host. Curious about middle-class ways, the six hosts follow Haruhi home one day and, after some comedic and heartfelt moments, they all sit down around Haruhi's small table to share a large pot of warm yosenabe. After all, nabe is best when eaten with people you care about.

- **4 cups Dashi Stock (page 56)**
- **¼ cup usukuchi light-colored soy sauce**
- **3 tablespoons sake**
- **2 tablespoons mirin**
- **½ pound pork belly, thinly sliced**
- **½ pound chicken thigh meat, boneless, cut into bite-size pieces**
- **1 bunch enoki mushrooms, root end discarded, separated into smaller bundles**
- **6 shiitake mushrooms, stems discarded**
- **1 leek, dark green top discarded, cut diagonally into 2-inch segments**
- **1 large carrot, peeled and sliced into ⅛-inch-thick discs**
- **½ package silken tofu, cut into 1-inch cubes**
- **½ package shirataki noodles, rinsed under very hot water and drained**
- **¼ head Napa cabbage, core removed, cut into 1½-inch segments**
- **1 bundle mizuna leaves or celery, leafy tops only**

1 In a large bowl, combine the dashi stock, soy sauce, sake, and mirin. In a large, wide pot or deep pan, position the pork belly, chicken, enoki and shiitake mushrooms, leek, carrot, tofu cubes, shiraki noodles, cabbage, and celery leaves in their own sections. Place the pot over medium heat and pour the prepared broth over the ingredients. Cover the pot and bring to a boil. Once boiling, turn the heat to medium-low and simmer, covered, until the vegetables are just tender.

2 Spoon the yosenabe into individual serving bowls. If you have a portable heating element, such as a hot plate, set it up on the dinner table and transfer the pot to it. Let the yosenabe simmer over low heat while family and friends gather around and use chopsticks to take what they'd like from the pot to add to their own individual bowls.

NOTES In *Ouran High School Host Club*, much to Tamaki's dismay, Haruhi says they will be having pork in the yosenabe because seafood and beef are too expensive. Thinly sliced beef and seafood like prawns or shrimp are common ingredients in yosenabe, as well as chicken meatballs and fishballs. Yosenabe is an anything-goes type of dish; you could add tomatoes, cheese, eggs, you name it!

After the meat and vegetables are eaten from the pot, it's common to put either cooked rice or udon or ramen noodles into the remaining broth and bring it back to a boil. This is called shime, which means "to finish up the meal." Putting rice in specifically, often with beaten egg, is known as zosui, and creates a type of rice porridge. It differs from Okayu (page 30) because zosui is cooked in broth instead of plain water.

FOOD FACTS The name yosenabe breaks down into *yose* meaning "to gather," as in gathering various ingredients, but can also mean gathering people to share the meal; and *nabe*, which is short for *nabemono*, which basically means "things in a pot," and is more commonly referred to as a one-pot dish. Nabe can also be named after the main meat featured in it, such as tori nabe for chicken, buta nabe for pork, etc.

There are several types of nabemono. Chanko nabe is loaded with protein-rich ingredients, such as chicken and fish, along with tofu and vegetables, and is a favorite of sumo wrestlers as seen in *Hinomaru Sumo*. Sukiyaki, like in *Princess Jellyfish* and *One-Punch Man*, often uses choice beef, which is commonly dipped in raw egg after cooking alongside veggies in soy, mirin, and sugar. There's shabu-shabu, named for the gentle sound of thin meat being swished in hot water, as seen in *Prison School*. Oden is a nabe of konnyaku, daikon, and fish cakes, among other ingredients, often sold by street vendors, and can be found in *Mr. Osomatsu*. Motsunabe is made with cabbage, garlic chives, and offal (animal organs), and can be seen in *Hakata Mentai! Pirikarako-chan* and *Hyakko*. And then there's yudofu, tofu cubes simmered in a simple kombu broth, as seen in *Bungo Stray Dogs* and *Isekai Izakaya: Japanese Food from Another World*.

THIS FOOD ALSO APPEARS IN . . .

- *Today's Menu for the Emiya Family*
- *The Eccentric Family*
- *Hidamari Sketch*
- *Urusei Yatsura*
- *Black Bullet*
- *Fighting Spirit (Hajime no Ippo)*
- *Love Live! Sunshine!!*
- *The Pet Girl of Sakurasou*
- *Himouto! Umaru-chan*
- *Elegant Yokai Apartment Life*
- *YuruYuri: Happy Go Lily*

PRINCESS MONONOKE

OKAYU

Rice Porridge

SERVES 2 On his journey to see, with eyes unclouded by hate, the root cause of the curse slowly devouring his arm—and the corruption of the great boar spirit that gave it to him—Prince Ashitaka meets the traveling monk Jigo, who shares with Ashitaka the warmth of his fire and a simple meal of okayu. Over the meal, Jigo tells Ashitaka that help may be obtained from the Great Forest Spirit near Iron Town.

½ cup cooked Rice (see page 52)

Salt

In a large pot, combine the rice and 3½ cups of water, then cover and bring to a boil. Stir well, cover again, then reduce the heat to low and allow to simmer, undisturbed, for 30 minutes. Remove the pot from the heat and let sit, still covered, for 10 minutes. Stir in salt to taste, if desired.

NOTES In *Princess Mononoke*, Jigo includes greens in his okayu. A leek—the pale green portion cut into 1-inch-by-¼-inch strips—a green onion, or a few chives are good additions; simply add them to the okayu before serving. The garlic chive variation is what Kyo served Tohru in *Fruits Basket* when she was sick!

Other yummy toppings include umeboshi (salted pickled plums, as seen in the photo), flaked Shiozake (page 14), salted kelp, and tsukemono like Pickled Daikon (page 72) and Kyuri Asazuke (page 81).

FOOD FACTS There is a type of okayu called nanakusa gayu that included seven different greens for extra medicinal benefit, such as chickweed, cudweed, turnip and daikon radish greens, shepherd's purse, dropwort, and henbit. You can use other greens such as kale, spinach, swiss chard, collard greens, celery leaves, or flat-leaf parsley (as seen in the photo). If any are tough, simply blanch them in boiling water separately from the okayu to make them more tender, then put them in an ice bath to stop them from cooking. Nanakusa gayu can be eaten anytime, but is traditionally served on January 7, Jinjitsu or "Human Day," as a wish for one's good health in the upcoming year, and as a rest for the stomach after the previous six days of New Year feasting.

Another type of okayu is boiled with red beans and traditionally eaten on January 15, Koshogatsu or "Little New Year," to ward off evil spirits. Okayu is also used in an ancient ritual called kayu-ura on this day for regional agricultural divination. Chagayu is yet another type of okayu, boiled with hojicha green tea instead of water, eaten hot or chilled, and enjoyed by monks in ancient times. This tea okayu is different from chazuke (see page 33) because the rice is cooked with the tea as opposed to simply pouring the tea over rice that has already been cooked.

A dish called zosui may seem similar to okayu, but the former is rice cooked in broth and soy sauce—often the remaining stock of a nabemono (page 29)—whereas okayu is simply made with water.

THIS FOOD ALSO APPEARS IN . . .

- *Kiki's Delivery Service*
- *Gate*
- *Laughing Under the Clouds*
- *Kono Oto Tomare!: Sounds of Life*
- *Hinako Note*
- *March Comes in Like a Lion*
- *Hanasaku Iroha: Blossoms for Tomorrow*
- *My Wife Is the Student Council President*
- *New Game!*
- *Onihei*
- *Fruits Basket*

BUNGO STRAY DOGS

CHAZUKE

Tea or Broth Poured over Rice

SERVES 1 After being kicked out of the orphanage he grew up in, Atsushi Nakajima is weak and starving and dreams of eating comforting chazuke. In order to survive, he decides he'll have to steal from the next person he comes across, but the person he sees is upside down, drowning in the river. After saving the person's life, Atsushi is treated to a meal, and ends up eating so many bowls of chazuke that he practically pops out of his clothes.

- **1 tablespoon vegetable oil**
- **1/2 chicken breast or thigh, boneless, cut into bite-size pieces**
- **Pinch of salt, plus more to taste**
- **Pinch of freshly ground black pepper, plus more to taste**
- **2 teaspoons cornstarch**
- **1 cup cooked Rice (page 52)**
- **1 umeboshi (salted pickled plum)**
- **1 tablespoon shio kombu (salted kombu kelp) strips**
- **1 tablespoon small strips of roasted nori**
- **1 green onion, white and pale green parts chopped**
- **1 cup Green Tea (page 113), like sencha, hojicha, or genmaicha**

1 Heat the oil in a small pan over medium heat. Toss the chicken pieces with a pinch each of salt and pepper, then toss with the cornstarch. Squeeze each piece of chicken to compact the starch coating. Add the chicken to the pan and cook until browned and crispy all over, about 2 minutes per side. Remove to a paper towel and sprinkle with more salt and pepper, if desired.

2 Scoop the rice into a serving bowl and place the chicken around the sides. Top with the umeboshi, shio kombu, nori, and green onion. Pour the tea around the rice and enjoy.

FOOD FACTS The *cha* in chazuke refers to tea, while *zuke* means "to submerge." Chazuke is great for leftover rice and other ingredients like Shiozake (page 14) and Karaage (page 66). Other ingredients can be added, such as Tempura (page 15), corn, pickles, salmon roe, furikake, green onions—whatever suits your tastes. Instead of tea, sometimes Dashi (page 56) or other broth is poured over the rice. You can even eat it cold, as mentioned in *Today's Menu for the Emiya Family.*

In *Kuma Miko: Girl Meets Bear,* Michi prepares cold-water rice called mizu kake gohan, which is similar to cold chazuke but uses plain water and ice cubes instead of tea or broth. It's lovely on a hot summer day! To make mizu gohan, rinse 1 cup of cooked rice in cold water and place it in a serving bowl. Pour 1 cup of cold water over the rice and add ice cubes around the sides. Top with cucumber slices, 1 teaspoon of shiro (white) miso, 1 to 2 chopped umeboshi (seeds removed), and a sprinkling of katsuobuchi bonito flakes. There's also another version in *Kuma Miko* that's Italian-inspired, with garlic, basil, cherry tomatoes, eggs, and bacon.

CULTURE FACTS In the past, in Kyoto, chazuke was referred to as bubuzuke and was offered to a guest as a signal that they had overstayed their welcome. Today, outside of Kyoto, this reference is sometimes used to tease those from Kyoto.

ANIME FACTS "Bungo," in the anime and manga title of *Bungo Stray Dogs,* translates to "literary language," which goes perfectly with all of the literary-named characters and literary allusions in the story.

THIS FOOD ALSO APPEARS IN . . .

- *Himouto! Umaru-chan*
- *Ms. Koizumi Loves Ramen Noodles*
- *Yotsuiro Biyori*
- *Food Wars!*
- *Golden Kamuy: OVA*
- *Gourmet Girl Graffiti*
- *Suite PreCure*
- *Today's Menu for the Emiya Family*

KAKURIYO: BED & BREAKFAST FOR SPIRITS

OYAKODON

Chicken and Egg Rice Bowl

SERVES 1 Whisked away to the spirit world by the handsome ogre Odanna, Aoi Tsubaki is told that she must marry him in order to pay off her grandfather's debt. Like her grandfather, Aoi has the ability to see and interact with ayakashi (supernatural beings), and, since she was very young, has been taught to make delicious meals—meals that ayakashi love! So, instead of marrying Odanna, she decides to go to work preparing meals for ayakashi in order to pay back the debt. As it turns out, Aoi's food has strong spiritual powers that can restore ayakashi energy.

1/2 large onion, julienned
1 pound chicken thighs or breasts, boneless, cut into bite-size pieces
1 teaspoon sugar
1/3 cup Dashi Stock (page 56)
1 tablespoon soy sauce
1 tablespoon mirin
1 tablespoon sake
2 eggs, lightly beaten
1 cup cooked Rice (see page 52)
1 green onion, pale green and white parts chopped
1 tablespoon fresh mizuna or flat-leaf parsley, chopped

1 In a small pan over medium heat, spread out the onion and chicken. Sprinkle the sugar on top and pour in the dashi, soy sauce, mirin, and sake. Bring to a boil, then cover and reduce heat to a gentle simmer for 5 minutes.

2 Pour the beaten eggs over the chicken and onion mixture, cover again, and turn off the heat. Let it steam until the egg is mostly set but still slightly runny, or until desired doneness. Slide the mixture onto a bowl of cooked rice and garnish with chopped green onion and mizuna or parsley.

FOOD FACTS The name oyakodon comes from the portmanteau *oyako* containing *ko* from *kodomo* meaning "child," plus *oya* meaning "parent," along with *don* from *donburi* for "rice bowl." So it literally means "parent and child rice bowl," because it's made with chicken and egg!

Typically oyakodon refers to chicken and egg as a rice topping, but another popular version uses salmon, either Shiozake (see page 14) or sashimi, and salmon roe (fish eggs).

CULTURE FACTS In a 1972 *Rolling Stone* interview, singer-songwriter Paul Simon said that the title of his song "Mother and Child Reunion" came from a Chinese menu with a dish of the same name. That dish, of course, was oyakodon, translated literally on the menu.

Ayakashi, *yokai*, and *mononoke* are all words that refer to supernatural beings in Japanese folklore. The differences are semantic, often subtle, and sometimes based on region, so the words are often used interchangeably to refer to supernatural beings in a broader sense. There are many, many specific names for these types of beings, though, that can be found throughout folklore, and thus anime and manga.

THIS FOOD ALSO APPEARS IN . . .

- *Sket Dance*
- *The Kawai Complex Guide to Manors & Hostel Behavior*
- *Food Wars!*
- *Toriko*
- *Inuyashiki*

TORADORA!

TONKATSU

Breaded and Fried Pork Cutlet

SERVES 2 Kind Ryuji Takasu struggles with the negative assumptions people make about him because of his intimidating eyes. Small but fiery Taiga Aisaka has a reputation for disliking everyone and snaps at people like a little tiger. Through a series of events, Ryuji and Taiga team up to get romantically closer to each other's best friends, causing the two to spend a lot of time together. Taiga often ends up at Ryuji's house, eating his tasty meals, like tonkatsu. Don't forget the sauce!

Vegetable or canola oil
2 pork loin cutlets, rinsed and patted dry
Salt and freshly ground black pepper
¼ cup all-purpose flour
1 egg, beaten
⅓ cup panko bread crumbs
2 cups thinly shredded green cabbage
Tonkatsu Sauce (recipe follows)

1 In a medium pan over medium heat, add 1 inch of oil and bring to 350°F. Meanwhile, lay the cutlets on a cutting board and make small cuts in any lines of fat so that the meat won't curl when cooking. Tenderize the cutlets using the back of a large knife, then shape the cutlets into ovals. Sprinkle lightly all over with salt and pepper.

2 Line up 3 shallow bowls: one with the flour, the next with the beaten egg, and the last with the panko. Coat the pork with flour, dip in the egg, then coat with panko, pressing gently so the crumbs stick well. Lay the cutlets in the hot oil and cook, flipping when needed, until browned and crispy on both sides, a total of about 5 minutes. Transfer to a paper-towel-lined plate.

3 Lay the cutlets on a cutting board and slice into 1-inch strips. Arrange the strips in a cutlet shape on a serving plate with the cabbage and drizzle with the tonkatsu sauce.

TONKATSU SAUCE

2 tablespoons ketchup
1 tablespoon Worcestershire sauce
1 tablespoon dark brown sugar
1 teaspoon mirin
1 teaspoon oyster sauce
½ teaspoon soy sauce

Whisk all of the ingredients together. Adjust seasoning to your taste, if needed.

FOOD FACTS Tonkatsu is a portmanteau of *ton* for "pig" and *katsu* from *katsuretsu* for "cutlet," but it is often made with chicken breast or thigh, as in *I Can't Understand What My Husband Is Saying*, or sometimes beefsteak, like in *Food Wars!*. The names change, though, to "torikatsu" and "gyukatsu," respectively.

Tonkatsu can be turned into Katsudon (page 36) by serving it on a bowl of rice with an egg mixture on top, or katsu curry by serving it on a plate of rice with curry sauce (see page 16) poured over top. In *Cheer Boys!!* we see tonkatsu served with fried rice (see page 55) and curry, and in *The Ryuo's Work is Never Done!*, we get Kanazawa-style katsu curry with rice hidden under darker sauce and tonkatsu on top, drizzled with tonkatsu sauce and a side of shredded cabbage.

Tonkatsu sandwiches, called "katsu sando," are a very popular item that can often be found in bento or "konbini" (convenience stores) in anime. You can see them in *Ranma ½*, *Gourmet Girl Graffiti*, *Mr. Tonegawa: Middle Management Blues*, *Isekai Izakaya: Japanese Food from Another World*, and more.

To make your own katsu sando, shape a breaded pork cutlet into the size and shape of a bread slice and fry the cutlet to make tonkatsu. Spread softened butter or mayonnaise on two slices of thick, fluffy white bread—or, better yet, a mixture of 1 tablespoon softened butter, ¼ teaspoon yellow mustard, and 1 teaspoon Kewpie mayonnaise. Spread a small amount of tonkatsu sauce on one of the slices, over the butter, and add a handful of shredded green cabbage (you can omit this if you don't like cabbage). Drizzle more tonkatsu sauce over the cabbage and place the tonkatsu cutlet on top. Spread tonkatsu sauce over the cutlet and then close the sandwich. At this point you can choose to cut the crusts from the bread or leave them on. Wrap the sandwich tightly in plastic wrap and let it sit for 5 minutes between two plates. To serve, use a long, sharp serrated knife to cut the sandwich in half, and set the halves next to each other with the cut sides facing up. You can leave the plastic wrap on for easy handling, or remove it.

CULTURE FACTS The term for Ryuji's intimidating eyes is *sanpaku*, meaning "three whites," and is used to describe eyes that show white space (sclera) not only to the right and left of the iris but also either above or below. It's thought that people with this condition either attract trouble or cause trouble to those around them. In anime, characters with sanpaku are often viewed as delinquents, thugs, or criminals, or are simply considered scary, as in poor Ryuji's case.

THIS FOOD ALSO APPEARS IN . . .

- *Elegant Yokai Apartment Life*
- *Prison School*
- *Samurai Flamenco*
- *Amagami SS*
- *Natsume's Book of Friends*
- *Future Diary*
- *A Certain Scientific Accelerator*
- *Tonkatsu DJ Agetaro*
- *Laid-Back Camp*
- *The Kawai Complex Guide to Manors & Hostel Behavior*
- *I've Always Liked You*
- *Your Name*
- *The Disastrous Life of Saiki K.*

YURI!!! ON ICE

KATSUDON

Pork Cutlet Rice Bowl

SERVES 1 In order to be coached by the famous Russian figure skater Viktor Nikiforov, troubled figure skater Yuri Katsuki is presented with the challenge of skating to the theme of eros in an ice-skating face-off, and declares emphatically that he will embody a tasty pork cutlet bowl. Katsudon is Yuri's all-time favorite food, and the desire to eat it is the only way he can fathom the concept of passionate love, though the drive to win so that he can be by Viktor's side is indicative of a grander passion than pork cutlets could ever evoke.

- **1 to 1½ cups cooked Rice (see page 52)**
- **1 recipe Tonkatsu (page 35)**
- **¼ cup Dashi Broth (page 56)**
- **1 tablespoon mirin**
- **1½ teaspoons soy sauce**
- **1½ teaspoons sugar**
- **¼ large onion, julienned**
- **1 large egg, beaten**
- **1 tablespoon peas, thawed if frozen (optional)**

1 Place the rice in a serving bowl large enough for the tonkatsu to sit on top of the rice, then set aside until needed. Slice the tonkatsu into ½-by-¾-inch strips and have ready near the stove. In a small pan over medium heat, combine the dashi broth, mirin, soy sauce, and sugar. Add the onion and toss to coat. Cover and simmer until the sugar is dissolved and the onion is tender, about 5 minutes.

2 Lay the sliced tonkatsu on top of the onions in the pan and let the meat cook for a minute to heat through. Pour the beaten egg over the tonkatsu and cover to steam the egg for 1 minute until half-set, or to your desired doneness.

3 Remove the pan from the heat and slide the contents directly onto your waiting bowl of rice. Top with the peas, if using, and you're ready to eat!

FOOD FACTS Katsudon, said to have originated around Waseda University in Shinjuku, Tokyo, in the early 1900s, is a portmanteau of *tonkatsu* for "pork cutlet" and *donburi* for "rice bowl." This dish is a great way to use up leftover tonkatsu. It can also be made with chicken katsu or even beef katsu, like in *Food Wars!*.

The "katsu" in "katsudon" is a homophone of the *katsu* that means "victory" in Japanese. This makes it perfect for Yuri (whose last name just happens to be *Katsuki*), and also helps us understand why it's Deku's favorite food in *My Hero Academia*. Many people in Japan eat katsudon before a big event—for example, students before a test—hoping for victory. Any food with "katsu" will do!

ANIME FACTS *Yuri!!! on Ice* is filled with food. Just look at the eye-catch cards (intermission bumpers)! If you pay attention, you can see that they are meaningful for each episode. Even the gifts fans throw to Yuri on the ice are often food plushies. A very memorable food in the series is the katsudon piroshki, a fusion food that Yuri's grandfather makes after hearing that Yuri enjoyed the katsudon he had while in Japan. Piroshki, sometimes spelled pirozhki, are savory buns, either baked or fried, from Eastern Europe. In a subtle way the katsu-roshki are a marker of Yuri's personal growth.

THIS FOOD ALSO APPEARS IN . . .

- *My Hero Academia*
- *Hozuki's Coolheadedness*
- *Future Diary*
- *Gate*
- *March Comes in Like a Lion*
- *Free! Dive to the Future*
- *The Devil Is a Part-Timer!*
- *Hitorijime My Hero*
- *Yu-Gi-Oh! Zexal*
- *Honey and Clover*

PERSONA 4: THE ANIMATION

GYUDON

Beef Rice Bowl

SERVES 1 Conquering this dish requires understanding, knowledge, courage, and dedication.

- **1 large onion, julienned**
- **2 teaspoons sugar**
- **½ cup Dashi Stock (page 56)**
- **2 tablespoons mirin**
- **2 tablespoons soy sauce**
- **1 tablespoons sake**
- **½ pound beef, sliced into $\frac{1}{16}$-inch strips**
- **1 cup cooked Rice (see page 52)**
- **1 large egg, at room temperature (optional)**

1 In a medium pan over medium heat, toss the onions with sugar, then stir in the dashi stock, mirin, soy sauce, and sake. Add in the beef, stirring frequently, and cook until the meat is no longer red, 5 to 7 minutes. Reduce the heat to a simmer, cover, and cook for 10 minutes. Slide the meat mixture onto a bowl of rice to serve.

2 If you'd like to put an egg on top, as seen in *Persona 4*, separate the yolk and white of the egg and pour the white onto the meat mixture in the pan for the last minute to cook. Place the rice in a bowl, top with the meat mixture, and make a small well at the center top. Gently plop the yolk into the well and enjoy!

NOTES It's recommended to use a pasteurized egg in this recipe, but if you can't find any in the store, you can make your own: Place an egg in a medium pot, cover with water, and, using a digital or candy thermometer, bring the temperature to a steady 140°F for 3 minutes. If it starts to go over, adjust the heat or pour in a bit more water to bring the temperature down. Rinse the egg under cold water and use as directed. If you'd rather not go the egg route, beni shoga (pickled ginger) is also a common topping for gyudon.

ANIME FACTS In *Yu-Gi-Oh!* there is a restaurant called Gyudon Yaro, which translates to Beef Bowl Buster. *Gyu* means "beef" and *don* is short for *donburi*. *Yaro* historically meant "man," but in modern times is used more as a slang word for "dude" or, depending on your tone, could even mean "jerk." *Buster* is a form of address in American slang—as in "Listen here, Buster . . ." —that's a bit dated now, but in the Gyudon Yaro context it can also mean that you're gonna bust up that beef bowl because it's so good!

THIS FOOD ALSO APPEARS IN . . .

- *Steins;Gate*
- *Nichijou—My Ordinary Life*
- *Food Wars!*
- *Silver Spoon*
- *Senryu Girl*
- *Moribito: Guardian of the Spirit*
- *Beyond the Boundary*
- *Dropkick on My Devil!*
- *Red Data Girl*
- *Yozakura Quartet*
- *Yu-Gi-Oh!*
- *Tari Tari*

THE GARDEN OF WORDS

OMURICE

Fried Rice Omelet

SERVES 1 The drenched mornings of the rainy season bring them together under a park gazebo: a student who dreams of becoming a shoemaker and a mysterious woman who eats chocolates and quotes ancient poetry. They're both taking refuge from a world that pushes against them and find solace in each other's company. Getting caught in the rain one morning brings them both to the lady's home, where the young man prepares a comforting meal of omurice while their clothes dry.

- **2 tablespoons vegetable or canola oil**
- **½ cup minced onion**
- **2 tablespoons ketchup, plus more for drizzling**
- **3½ tablespoons chicken stock**
- **½ tablespoon soy sauce**
- **¾ cup cooked Rice (see page 52)**
- **2 large eggs**
- **1 teaspoon minced fresh flat-leaf parsley**

1 Heat 1 tablespoon of oil in a medium pan over medium heat. Add the onion, stirring often, and cook until soft and just beginning to caramelize, about 8 minutes. Stir in the ketchup, 1½ tablespoons of the chicken stock, and the soy sauce. Fold in the rice until fully combined and cook until heated through. Remove the pan from the heat and use a spatula to shape the rice into a compact log.

2 In another medium pan over medium heat, spread the remaining tablespoon of oil to coat the bottom of the pan. Whisk the eggs in a bowl with the remaining 2 tablespoons of chicken stock, then pour the mixture into the pan. Swirl the pan so the egg mixture spreads out evenly. Cook until the bottom is set but the top is still slightly runny, about 2 minutes. Lay the rice log into the center of the egg mixture and use a spatula or two to fold the sides over the rice, tapping them gently into place. Remove the pan from the heat.

3 Move the omelet to one side of the pan, hold the pan against the edge of a serving plate, and gently slide and flip the omelet over onto the plate. Tuck any egg edges under the omelet and reshape as needed. Drizzle ketchup over the omurice and sprinkle with minced flat-leaf parsley.

NOTES Using a paper towel or plastic wrap can help shape the omurice once it's on the plate, before the ketchup drizzle. Sometimes ketchup bottles can squeeze out messily, so for a more controlled and thin flow, scoop some ketchup into a plastic sandwich bag, seal, and snip a tiny hole in one corner, then drizzle away!

The omurice in *The Garden of Words* is very tasty, but also very simple in ingredients. Other common ingredients are minced carrot, cooked with the onions; bite-size chicken, added after the onions are tender; and peas and corn, folded in when the rice is added. Other toppings in place of ketchup include Tonkatsu Sauce (page 35), curry (page 16), demi-glace, and gravy. Instead of wrapping the cooked egg around the rice, you can also lay an egg pillow on top of the rice and slice it down the center to let it fall open. This version is called fuwatoro omurice, from *fuwa fuwa* meaning "fluffy" and *toro toro* meaning "runny." We see this type in *Blue Exorcist: The Movie* and *Gourmet Girl Graffiti*.

FOOD FACTS *Omu* in *omurice* comes from the Japanese pronunciation of omelet, "omuretsu."

You can often find omurice in anime with messages or pictures drawn on top in ketchup, as in *Hanasaku Iroha*, *Charlotte*, and *After the Rain*. This is also a common practice at maid cafés in Japan—the hostesses often take requests from the patrons and do the ketchup art at the table, like in *Maid-Sama!* and *Outbreak Company*.

THIS FOOD ALSO APPEARS IN . . .

- *Star Driver*
- *Mob Psycho 100*
- *Blue Exorcist: The Movie*
- *Gundam Build Fighters*
- *Gourmet Girl Graffiti*
- *Shirobako*
- *Junjo Romantica*
- *Monthly Girls' Nozaki-Kun*
- *Hanasaku Iroha: Blossoms for Tomorrow*
- *Charlotte*
- *After the Rain*

COWBOY BEBOP

CHINJAO ROSU

Steak and Bell Pepper Stir-Fry

SERVES 2 Bounty hunters in space! With humanity settling the stars, crime has spread all over the galaxy. If you need to earn some cash, why not round up some of those n'er-do-wells? Jet Black, owner of the ship *Bebop*, is good at many things, including cooking. He often makes chinjao rosu for himself and his partner, Spike Spiegel, though it always ends up being a "poor man's" version of the dish because they have no money for meat after paying off all the damages Spike incurs when collecting his bounties.

- **1/2 pound beefsteak, cut into 1/4-inch-by-2-inch strips, 1/8 inch or less thick**
- **4 teaspoons sake**
- **2 teaspoons soy sauce**
- **2 teaspoons cornstarch**
- **1 teaspoon oyster sauce**
- **1/2 teaspoon sugar**
- **1/2 teaspoon finely grated garlic**
- **1/2 teaspoon finely grated ginger**
- **1 teaspoon sesame oil**
- **3/4 cup green bell pepper, core and seeds discarded, cut into 1/4-inch-by-2-inch strips**
- **3/4 cup boiled bamboo, drained and cut into 1/4-inch-wide strips**

1 In a bowl, combine the meat strips with 2 teaspoons sake, 1 teaspoon soy sauce, and 1 teaspoon cornstarch and set aside. In another bowl, stir together the remaining 2 teaspoons sake, 1 teaspoon soy sauce, and 1 teaspoon cornstarch with the oyster sauce, sugar, garlic, and ginger and set aside as well.

2 Heat the sesame oil in a large pan over medium heat and sauté the bell peppers and bamboo until the peppers are just tender, about 2 minutes. Stir in the meat and cook until it's no longer red, 5 to 7 minutes. Pour in the sauce and fold everything together to coat and cook through. Serve your chinjao rosu as is or alongside rice, or even in a bento.

NOTE If you'd like to keep the dish authentic to *Cowboy Bebop*, or prefer a vegetarian version, omit the beef and its marinade. Increase the amount of bell pepper and bamboo to compensate. To add more color, you can use different types of bell peppers.

FOOD FACTS Originating in China, chinjao rosu, meaning "peppers" and "shredded meat," has been adapted to Japanese tastes by using different seasonings and beef instead of the traditional pork. In other parts of the world, like the United States, it's often simply referred to as pepper steak. Chinjao rosu is an example of chuka ryori, or Chinese food in Japan.

ANIME FACTS Chinjao rosu is the favorite dish of Don Chinjao, a former pirate captain and head of the Chinjao family, in the anime *One Piece*.

THIS FOOD ALSO APPEARS IN . . .

- *The Story of Saiunkoku*
- *Food Wars!*
- *One Piece*
- *True Cooking Master Boy*
- *Flavors of Youth*

NAPOLITAN

Spaghetti with Ketchup Sauce

SERVES 1 While getting his lunch in the cafeteria one day, cool, clever, and capable Sakamoto hears from the lunch lady that no one has been interested in the spaghetti napolitan she just added to the menu. In response, Sakamoto creates split-second, squiggly subliminal messages during his activities at school, and the next day everyone is enjoying napolitan for lunch!

- **1/4 teaspoon salt**
- **2 ounces uncooked spaghetti noodles**
- **2 tablespoons ketchup**
- **1/2 teaspoon Worcestershire sauce**
- **1/4 teaspoon sugar**
- **1 to 2 drops Tabasco sauce (optional)**
- **2 tablespoons unsalted butter**
- **1 slice thick-cut bacon, cut into 1/2-inch pieces**
- **1/4 large onion, julienned 1/4 inch wide**
- **1/2 teaspoon minced garlic**
- **1/4 large green bell pepper, stem and core removed, cut into 2-by-1/4-inch strips**
- **1/2 teaspoon vegetable or canola oil**
- **Grated parmesan cheese (optional)**

1 In a large pot, bring 4 cups of water and salt to a boil. Add the noodles, unbroken, and swirl them down into the water once they soften enough. Boil for 10 to 12 minutes, then drain, reserving 2 tablespoons of the cooking liquid. Place the noodles back in the pot, with the heat turned off.

2 In a small bowl, whisk together the ketchup, reserved noodle liquid, Worcestershire sauce, sugar, Tabasco sauce (if using), and butter. Pour the mixture over the noodles and toss to combine.

3 In a large pan over medium heat, cook the bacon, stirring occasionally, for 2 minutes. Stir in the onion and garlic and toss with the oil. Cook, stirring often, until the onions are just tender, about 3 minutes. Add the bell pepper and cook for another 2 minutes.

4 Fold the bacon, onion, and pepper mixture into the spaghetti and cook over medium heat for about 2 minutes to evaporate any extra moisture as needed to reach your desired sauce consistency. Remove from the heat and serve with grated parmesan and extra Tabasco sauce on the side.

NOTE Mushrooms and smoked sausages are very common inclusions in napolitan. Add four white mushrooms, sliced 1/4 inch thick, and one long smoked sausage, cut diagonally, also 1/4 inch thick, along with the onions and peppers. If you're using sausage, you don't *need* to use bacon, but it's fine if you do! Using different-colored bell peppers is a visually appealing option, and sometimes a fried egg is added on top for more color. Eggplant slices are occasionally added, too, as seen in *Penguin Highway*. *Kakuriyo: Bed & Breakfast for Spirits* gives us a unique take on napolitan by adding meatballs and using udon noodles instead of spaghetti.

FOOD FACTS The leading theory of the origin of spaghetti napolitan is that it was created at the Hotel New Grand in Yokohama in 1950s postwar Japan by chef Irie Shigetada. The hotel had been transformed into temporary living quarters for the American military at that point, and it is said that Chef Irie was inspired by the soldiers' spaghetti rations. Sometime later, after the dish's popularity had spread, ketchup and smoked sausages were used, as they were more accessible and affordable ingredients. Perhaps the dish was called napolitan because Chef Irie's original ingredients may have resembled an Italian neapolitan ragu, or maybe the name napolitan simply sounded fancy!

This is a prime example of the yoshoku, or Western-influenced food culture, prevalent in Japan, as spaghetti napolitan went on to become popular all over the country.

CULTURE FACTS The Japanese company Kagome Co., founded in 1899 and specializing in tomato-based products like ketchup, created the napolitan-inspired female mascot Napoli-tan, whose wish is to fill your heart and stomach with tasty napolitan!

THIS FOOD ALSO APPEARS IN . . .

- *Yuri Bear Storm*
- *Yotsuiro Biyori*
- *How Heavy are the Dumbbells you Lift?*
- *Penguin Highway*
- *Isekai Izakaya: Japanese Food from Another World*
- *Food Wars!*
- *Good Luck Girl!*
- *Love, Chunibyo & Other Delusions!*
- *Aquarion Evol*
- *Glasslip*
- *Free! Dive to the Future*
- *The Disappearance of Nagato Yuki-chan*
- *Mr. Osomatsu*

HUNTER X HUNTER

SPAGHETTI BOLOGNESE

Spaghetti with Meat Sauce

SERVES 2 Could you finish a huge plate of this in thirty minutes? Gon and Kilua can—in half the time, even—especially for a free meal and a Galgaida card! But oops—they don't have any money to pay for their sodas . . .

2 teaspoons olive oil
1/4 large onion, minced
1 teaspoon minced garlic
1/4 pound ground beef, or a combination of ground beef and ground pork
1/4 cup finely grated carrot
5 large white mushrooms, sliced 1/4 inch thick
2 large tomatoes, diced
Pinch of sugar
Pinch of freshly ground black pepper
1/2 cup white wine or vegetable broth
1 tablespoon tomato paste
1/2 teaspoon Worcestershire sauce
1 bay leaf
1/4 teaspoon salt
4 ounces uncooked spaghetti noodles
1/2 tablespoon butter
1 teaspoon minced fresh flat-leaf parsley (optional)
Grated parmesan cheese (optional)

1 In a large pan over medium heat, combine the olive oil, onion, and garlic, and cook until just tender, about 4 minutes. Add the meat and break it into tiny pieces as it cooks. When the meat is no longer pink, mix in the carrot, mushrooms, tomatoes, sugar, and pepper and cook until heated through.

2 Whisk together the wine or broth, tomato paste, and Worcestershire sauce, then pour it into the pan, stirring to combine well. Add in the bay leaf, cover, and reduce the heat to low. Simmer for 30 minutes.

3 In a large pot, bring 4 cups water and the salt to a boil. Add the noodles, unbroken, and swirl them down into the water once they soften enough. Boil for 10 to 12 minutes, then drain.

4 Discard the bay leaf from the meat sauce and stir in the butter. Plate the spaghetti noodles and spoon the sauce on top. For optional garnish, sprinkle with the flat-leaf parsley and serve with grated parmesan cheese on the side.

FOOD FACTS Bolognese sauce is a ragu originating in Bologna, Italy. It traditionally uses tagliatelle noodles instead of spaghetti and is mixed in with the noodles instead of being served on top. There are other differences, but spaghetti Bolognese, often simply called spaghetti with meat sauce, is yet another example of food adaptation and fusion.

ANIME FACTS The spaghetti with a side of sodas (and subsequent dish washing) in the Greed Island arc of *Hunter x Hunter* is found in the manga and the anime adaptation that began in 1999, but not in the adaptation that started in 2011.

Elsewhere in the series, Kilua can be seen eating spaghetti mixed with tomato sauce, fresh cherry tomatoes cut in half, and sliced black olives, topped with fresh basil.

THIS FOOD ALSO APPEARS IN . . .

- *The Horizon*
- *Porco Rosso*
- *Recovery of an MMO Junkie*
- *After the Rain*
- *Amnesia*
- *Cardcaptor Sakura: Clear Card*
- *Shirobako*
- *Mister Ajikko*
- *Toradora SOS!*
- *I Can't Understand What My Husband Is Saying*
- *Restaurant to Another World*

TODAY'S MENU FOR THE EMIYA FAMILY

HAMBAGU

Ground Meat Patty with Sauce

SERVES 4 In a timeline where the Fifth Holy Grail War has ended and many of the participants have become friends, Shirou Emiya reminisces about the first time he made hambagu steak to make Kiritsugu Emiya, the man who rescued and raised him, proud. Now Shirou makes hambagu, and many other delicious meals, for family and friends sharing peaceful times together.

- **1 tablespoon vegetable or canola oil**
- **1 large onion, finely diced, divided**
- **Pinch plus 1/2 teaspoon salt**
- **1 pound ground beef, or a combination of beef and pork**
- **1 large egg**
- **1/3 cup panko bread crumbs**
- **1/4 teaspoon ground nutmeg**
- **1/4 teaspoon freshly ground black pepper**
- **1/4 cup red wine or beef broth**

FOR THE HAMBAGU SAUCE

- **1/4 cup red wine, chilled**
- **1/4 cup beef broth, chilled**
- **1/4 cup ketchup**
- **3 tablespoons Worcestershire sauce**
- **1 teaspoon brown sugar**
- **1 tablespoon butter**

1 In a large pan coated with the oil over medium heat, saute half of the diced onion with a pinch of salt, stirring often, until tender and caramelized, 4 to 5 minutes. Transfer the onions to a large plate and spread them out, then place them in the refrigerator to cool until needed.

2 Put the ground meat in a bowl with 1/2 teaspoon salt and quickly mix with your hands. Add the cooled onions, the remaining uncooked onions, the egg, panko, nutmeg, and pepper and mix again with your hands until thoroughly combined. Form the mixture into a ball and divide into 4 equal portions. Toss each portion back and forth between your hands several times to remove the air, then shape into 1-inch-thick oval patties. Lay the patties on a large plate, press an indentation in the center of each, then chill them in the refrigerator for 30 minutes.

3 Heat a large pan over medium heat and lay the patties in the pan once it's hot. Fry the patties until a crust forms on the bottom, about 5 minutes. Reduce the heat to medium-low and flip the patties. Pour in the red wine or beef broth and cover the pan to steam for 5 minutes. Uncover, turn the heat back up to medium, and let any residual liquid evaporate. Using a skewer or toothpick, poke one of the patties in the center; if the juices run clear, the patties are done. Increase the heat to high and cook for an additional 15 seconds, then reduce to medium. Transfer the patties to serving plates and cover with foil until ready to serve.

4 After removing the patties from the pan, make the sauce: Add the wine, broth, ketchup, Worcestershire sauce, and brown sugar to the pan. Whisk until well combined and smooth. Reduce the heat to medium-low and let the mixture simmer until thickened, about 3 minutes, stirring occasionally and skimming off any foam that arises. Add the butter and whisk it in until completely melted. Divide the sauce over the hambagu patties and serve.

FOOD FACTS Hambagu, sometimes referred to as hambagu steak, is the Japanese adaptation of Salisbury steak, which itself is a variation of the hamburger steak made popular in the United States by Russian and German immigrants from Hamburg, Germany, during the 1800s. The dish was brought to Japan by immigrants to the port of Yokohama in the late 1800s to early 1900s.

CULTURE FACTS In Hawaii, a place heavily influenced by Japanese culture because of immigration in the late 1800s, a variation of the Japanese hambagu steak called loco moco is served atop rice with a sunny-side-up egg. You can see this dish in *Food Wars!* and *HappinessCharge PreCure!*. It was created in the 1940s, originally without the egg, and named loco—Spanish for "crazy"—from the nickname of one of the boys who requested it, plus moco, simply because it was a fun rhyming word.

ANIME FACTS Hambagu is a popular *yoshoku*, or Western-influenced, food, usually served with a side of vegetables. It sometimes comes with a fried egg on top, as seen in *Fruits Basket* when Tohru gives Kyo a special serving, and with Nori's "hanamaru hambagu" in *Rozen Maiden*, in which the fried egg is flower-shaped to represent the Japanese *hanamaru* ("good job") mark for children (also known as a flower circle). In *My Love Story!!* there's even hambagu topped with pineapple rings!

THIS FOOD ALSO APPEARS IN . . .

- *Flying Witch*
- *Sweetness & Lightning*
- *Bunny Drop*
- *Clannad After Story*
- *Fresh Pretty Cure!*
- *Place to Place*
- *Akame ga Kill!*
- *Erased*
- *Aikatsu!*
- *Starmyu*
- *Hello!! Kinmoza!*
- *Cute High Earth Defense Club LOVE!*
- *Tokyo ESP*
- *Future Diary*
- *Cardfight!! Vanguard*
- *The Eccentric Family*
- *Aldnoah.Zero*
- *My Love Story!!*
- *Fruits Basket*
- *Rozen Maiden*
- *Food Wars!*
- *HappinessCharge PreCure!*

TWO

SIDES & BENTO

HAIKYU!!

RICE

SERVES 2 **Short but fearless, Shoyo Hinata dreams of playing high school volleyball with a real team on a real court. After years of practicing as best he can, he finally makes it and continues to play to his utmost. He chows down with vigor during mealtimes to regain his energy, scarfing mouthfuls of piled-high rice at breakfast.**

1 cup short-grain white rice

1 Place the rice in a large bowl and cover with cold water. Rub the rice grains with your fingers and between your hands for about 30 seconds, until the water turns milky. Strain the rice through a fine-mesh strainer and return to the bowl. Repeat this rubbing and rinsing process 4 to 5 times, until the water is almost clear.

2 Let the rice drain in the fine-mesh strainer for at least 15 minutes. Return the rice to the bowl, cover with cold water, and let soak for at least 30 minutes, or even as long as overnight. After the soaking, strain the rice one more time.

3 If you're using a rice cooker, pour the rice into the bowl of the cooker, cover with 1¼ cups of water—or the amount recommended by the rice cooker—and then continue to follow the cooker's instructions. Alternatively, if you're cooking the rice on the stovetop, transfer the rice to a large pot with a secure lid. Cover the rice with 1¼ cups water, then cover the pot with the lid. Bring to a boil over high heat. Don't lift the lid to peek—simply listen for the bubbling sound if the pot doesn't have a glass lid to see through. Reduce the heat to a low simmer and cook for another 5 to 7 minutes, or until you hear a hissing sound, meaning all of the water has been absorbed. You can peek quickly if you need to!

4 Turn off the heat but leave the pot where it is, covered, for 10 minutes to steam. Then remove the lid and use a rice paddle or fork to fold the bottom and top rice together, making sure not to stir and mush the grains. Now it's ready to serve. Lightly wetting the rice paddle or back of a spoon will help to shape a mound of rice in a bowl if that's how you'd like to serve it. Or, if you'd like to serve a mound of rice on a plate, you can pack the rice into a small bowl and then overturn it onto the plate.

NOTES A rice cooker cup actually equals ¾ of a regular cup measurement, so make sure that you use equivalent measuring cups for both your rice and water.

Rubbing and rinsing the rice is called polishing and gets rid of the extra starch. Polishing, draining, and soaking the rice gives each grain a chance to shine in the finished dish.

FOOD FACTS Japanese rice is short-grain and comes in two main categories: uruchimai, sometimes called sushi rice outside of Japan, which is an ordinary, non-glutinous rice used in many dishes including sake rice wine; and then there's mochigome, which is glutinous rice used for making such foods as mochi and senbei.

Kome is the Japanese word for rice, but often *gohan* is used to denote cooked rice (though gohan can also simply mean "meal"). Gohan, of course, is also the name of Goku's son in *Dragon Ball Z*, following along with the many food-based names in the series. *Meshi* is another Japanese word for rice, but it is more commonly used to refer to food in general.

Shoyo Hinata's favorite way to eat rice is by mixing raw egg with soy sauce into his bowl of rice. This is known as tamago kake gohan, "egg-splashed rice," and can be seen in *Silver Spoon* as well. Tamago kake gohan is a type of maze gohan, a category of rice dishes where ingredients are mixed in with already cooked rice. Another category is takikomi gohan, in which uncooked rice is cooked with seasonings and vegetables or meats mixed in. Examples of this can be found in *Dororo* with kuri gohan ("chestnut rice") and *Elegant Yokai Apartment Life* with kinoko gohan ("mushroom rice"). A third category of rice dishes is Chahan or fried rice (page 55): cooked rice stir-fried with seasonings and various ingredients. Chahan can be seen in *Weathering with You* and *True Cooking Master Boy*.

CULTURE FACTS Rice is deeply rooted in Japanese culture and has been a staple for thousands of years. It is not only polite to eat each grain of rice you are served, but folklore teaches that each grain of rice contains seven gods (seven being a lucky number in Japan) and that leaving any rice behind would offend them. So, for good luck, you'd better clean your bowl!

ANIME FACTS Did you know that there is an anime series about different varieties of Japanese rice? It's called *Love Rice* and focuses on anthropomorphized rice boys trying to show their school that rice is better than bread!

THIS FOOD ALSO APPEARS IN . . .

- *Sweetness & Lightning*
- *From Up on Poppy Hill*
- *Dragon Ball*
- *Elegant Yokai Apartment Life*
- *Mushi-Shi The Next Passage*
- *Non Non Biyori*
- *HappinessCharge PreCure!*
- *K-On!*
- *Love Rice*
- *True Tears*
- *Natsume's Book of Friends*
- *Urusei Yatsura*
- *Prison School*
- *A Bridge to the Starry Skies*
- *Inuyasha*
- *The Helpful Fox Senko-san*

THE HELPFUL FOX SENKO-SAN

INARIZUSHI

Seasoned Fried Tofu Stuffed with Sushi Rice

SERVES 2 The negative energy emanating from severely overworked salaryman Kuroto Nakano is so strong that it's enough to attract the attention of three kitsune in the spirit world, prompting the youngest—eight-hundred-year-old Senko—to move to Earth to pamper Kuroto in the hopes that his darkness will dissipate. Senko cooks and cleans and tends to Kuroto every day, reminding him to put self-care ahead of his demanding work.

2 pieces aburaage fried tofu

1/2 cup Dashi Stock (page 56)

1 tablespoon granulated sugar

2 teaspoons soy sauce

FOR THE SUSHI RICE

1 tablespoon plain rice vinegar

1 1/2 teaspoons sugar

1/4 teaspoon salt

1 cup cooked, still-hot, Rice (see page 52)

1 Bring 2 cups of water to a boil. Place the aburaage into a strainer and slowly pour the boiled water over them to remove any excess oil. Gently squeeze the aburaage, pat with a paper towel, and cut in half to get 4 squares.

2 In a medium pot over medium-high heat, bring the dashi to a low boil. Stir in the sugar and soy sauce. Reduce the heat to medium and submerge the aburaage pieces in the marinade. Let cook, stirring occasionally, until the liquid has been absorbed and evaporated, about 15 minutes. Remove from the heat and let the aburaage cool enough to handle.

3 Meanwhile, make the sushi rice: Combine the vinegar, sugar, and salt in a small bowl and cover with plastic wrap. Microwave for 1 minute to dissolve the sugar. Stir and microwave for 30 seconds more if the sugar is not yet dissolved.

4 Scoop the freshly cooked rice into a large, wide dish and use a rice paddle to separate it into an even layer. Pour the vinegar mixture over the rice and use the edge of the rice paddle to cut and fold the rice to mix the seasoning in evenly. Make sure not to press on the rice as you're mixing.

5 Wet your hands and divide the sushi rice into 4 equal pieces, forming each into a compact oblong shape. Squeeze the aburaage gently again and pat with a paper towel. Carefully open each piece on the cut end to create a pouch. Press 1 rice piece into each pouch and fold the sides of the opening over the rice to close. Place on a plate, seam side down, and repeat with the other pieces of aburaage and rice.

NOTE If you can't find plain aburaage or don't have the time to prepare them, you can find pre-seasoned aburaage, or "inari age," in many grocery stores. Simply follow this recipe from step 3 onward.

FOOD FACTS Inarizushi is also called inari sushi or oinari-san, and the latter is also a nickname given to the shrine to which these pouches often serve as offerings. There are different styles of inarizushi, such as a triangle to represent a fox ear, a rectangle that can be seen as a head with two fox ears, and a bag gathered at the top like a bag of grain, and sometimes the pouches are served open side up. Rice is the main ingredient, but variations exist, like mixing in sesame seeds or, as in *March Comes in Like a Lion*, mixing in wasabi and adding a scrambled egg and seasoned ground chicken. You can get very creative with these little pouches!

Other dishes that use aburaage are kitsune oden, kitsune udon, and kitsune soba, *kitsune* being the Japanese word for "fox." Fear not: There is no fox in these dishes; they are simply meals that a fox might like to eat because of the fried tofu! Thin strips of aburaage are also common in miso soup, and at festivals you can get thicker, grilled aburaage on a stick.

CULTURE FACTS These rice-filled tofu pouches received their name because they're associated with Inari Okami, the Shinto deity of agriculture and prosperity. Inari's messengers are fox spirits, and, at one point in antiquity, it was discovered that foxes like fried tofu. Historically, foxes helped rice farmers by eating the rodents that tried to eat their harvested grains, so foxes were a perfect fit as Inari's helpers. You'll find statues of fox spirits at Inari's shrines, as they are believed to relay human wishes to the deity.

Kitsune in folklore are a type of yokai, or supernatural creature, and have been portrayed as clever, wise, loyal, and at times mischievous and destructive. They have the ability to shape-shift into human form and advance in intelligence and power the older they get. The number of tails a kitsune spirit has signifies their age—nine being the most tails at one thousand years, known as a *kyubi no kitsune*. There are so many anime with kitsune, such as *Naruto*, *Inuyasha*, *Our Home's Fox Deity*, *Inari Kon Kon*, *Kamisama Kiss*, *Gugure! Kokkuri-san*, *Gingitsune: Messenger Fox of the Gods*, *Ushio and Tora*, *Yu Yu Hakusho*, *The Morose Mononokean*, and *Sonic the Hedgehog*, just to name a few!

THIS FOOD ALSO APPEARS IN . . .

- *Hiiro no Kakera: The Tamayori Princess Saga*
- *Gourmet Girl Graffiti*
- *Kakuriyo: Bed and Breakfast for Spirits*
- *March Comes in Like a Lion*
- *Food Wars!*
- *Kuromukuro*
- *Sengoku Collection*
- *Alice & Zoroku*
- *Touken Ranbu: Hanamaru*
- *Majikoi: Oh! Samurai Girls*
- *Poco's Udon World*

WEATHERING WITH YOU

CHAHAN

Rice Fried with Various Ingredients

SERVES 1 Wind and rain and snow and sun; but mostly rain. Tokyo is beset by downpours, and rural runaway Hodaka Morishima is almost done in during a freak storm while arriving in the city by boat. He meets his soon-to-be-employer Keisuke Suga, and then the kind and mysterious girl Hina, who serves him her special potato-chip chahan and ramen noodle salad. The down-and-out Hadoka begins to work with Suga to uncover the reason behind the extreme weather and the strange legend of the "weather maiden" who may be able to stop it.

1/4 cup pea sprouts or bean seedlings, plus more for garnish

1 tablespoon sesame oil

1 teaspoon grated ginger

1/3 cup finely chopped onion

1 large egg, yolk and white separated

1 cup cooked Rice (see page 52)

1 teaspoon soy sauce

2 teaspoons chicken bouillon powder or consomme, or the flavor packet from an instant chicken ramen

1/3 cup crushed seaweed-flavored potato chips, plus whole or broken chips for garnish

1 Cut the root end from the pea sprouts and cut the sprouts into 1-inch segments.

2 In a large pan over medium heat, combine the sesame oil and ginger and stir until fragrant.

3 Add the onion and cook, stirring often, until soft, about 3 minutes. Whisk the egg white and pour it into the pan, stirring to break it into small bits as it solidifies. Add the rice, soy sauce, chicken flavoring, and sprouts. Stir to combine and cook until heated through and the moisture has evaporated. Stir in the crushed potato chips at the very end.

4 Scoop the chahan into a small bowl and press to compact. Invert the bowl onto a serving plate and tap to dislodge the chahan. Make an indentation on top of the chahan mound using the back of a spoon and gently slide the whole egg yolk into the indent. Surround the yolk with a ring of sprouts and place extra chips around the sides of the chahan.

NOTES It's recommended to use a pasteurized egg in this recipe, but if you can't find any in the store, you can make your own! Place the egg in a medium pot, cover with water, and, using a digital or candy thermometer, bring the temperature to a steady 140°F for 3 minutes. If it starts to go over, adjust the heat or pour in a bit more water to bring the temperature down. Rinse the egg under cold water and then use as directed.

Along with the potato-chip chahan, Hina also serves a simple ramen noodle salad. To make it you'll need 2 to 3 handfuls baby spinach, stems removed; half an English cucumber, cut into matchsticks; 4 cherry tomatoes, quartered; and half a package of uncooked instant ramen noodles, broken into bite-size pieces. For the dressing, stir together 2 tablespoons Kewpie mayonnaise, 1 tablespoon finely ground toasted white sesame seeds, 1 teaspoon soy sauce, and salt and pepper to taste.

CULTURE FACTS The little ghosty-looking weather doll is called a teru teru bozu and means "shine shine baldie" or "shiny-headed monk." The dolls are charms created out of cloth or paper and hung up the day before nice weather is wanted. If the sun comes out, some people draw a face onto the doll and even give it sake. But if the weather stays bad, the little teru teru bozu might get its head chopped off! The origins of the weather doll are unclear, but some say it's based on a weather-predicting monk who once promised a lord good weather, then was beheaded when the weather remained poor. There's even a traditional chant about this. Others say that the origin is actually a girl who was sacrificed to bring good weather and thwart a flood; she was sent out with a broom to sweep away the storm clouds. Other girls hung little dolls of her to show their gratitude, and over time the design evolved into what the teru teru bozu is today. *Weathering with You* alludes to many of these ideas.

To make an easy weather doll, tightly ball up a tissue and place it in the center of another tissue. Gather the loose tissue around the ball and tie a ribbon around the gathered bit to secure the ball in place. Use a needle and thread if you want to hang it up, and draw on a face if you'd like!

THIS FOOD ALSO APPEARS IN . . .

- *One Piece*
- *True Cooking Master Boy*
- *Fighting Foodons*
- *Today's Menu for the Emiya Family*
- *Case File n°221: Kabukicho*
- *Hozuki's Coolheadedness*
- *Blue Exorcist*
- *Food Wars!*
- *Squid Girl*
- *A Place Further Than the Universe*
- *Sakura Quest*
- *Mr. Tonegawa: Middle Management Blues*
- *Release the Spyce*
- *Phantom in the Twilight*
- *Kiznaiver*

EVANGELION: 2.0: YOU CAN (NOT) ADVANCE

MISO SOUP

Dashi Broth and Miso Paste Soup

SERVES 2 The planet has been devastated by the catastrophic Second Impact and the resulting geographical and geopolitical upheaval. Huge beings known as Angels walk the Earth, leaving destruction in their wake, and are fought by equally huge Evangelions, piloted by human NERV pilots. While visiting the Marine Research Organization for a supposed sociology field trip, young NERV pilot Shinji Ikari comforts fellow pilot Rei Ayanami with homemade miso soup during their lunch break, explaining that it will warm her up.

1 tablespoon dried wakame seaweed

1 cup hot water

2 cups Dashi Stock (recipe follows) or 1 teaspoon dashi granules plus 2 cups water

2 tablespoons miso paste

½ block silken tofu, cut into bite-size cubes

1 Soak the dried wakame seaweed in the hot water for 10 minutes to rehydrate. Bring the dashi stock to a simmer over medium-low heat, or heat 2 cups of water with the dashi granules until the granules have dissolved.

2 Scoop some of the dashi broth into a large ladle and, holding it over the pot, stir 1 tablespoon of the miso paste into the ladle until dissolved. Pour the mixture into the pot and stir to combine. Repeat this step with the remaining tablespoon of miso paste.

3 Drain the wakame seaweed and add it to the pot along with the tofu cubes. Simmer the soup for another minute, then serve.

DASHI STOCK

1 (4 x 4-inch) piece dried kombu kelp, gently wiped of any sand or dirt

1 packed cup of large katsuobushi dried fish flakes (also called bonito)

1 Add 3 cups of water and the kombu to a medium pot over medium-low heat and bring to a simmer. Once the kombu is softened, use kitchen scissors to cut several fringes into its sides. Cover the pot and let it simmer for 15 minutes, then remove the kombu to a paper towel to dry. The kombu can be used again to make a second dashi later—store in the freezer in an airtight container. It can also be used to make furikake rice seasoning or tsukudani (see below).

2 Increase the heat to medium to bring the liquid to a low boil and add the katsuobushi flakes. Cook, uncovered, for another 2 minutes, stirring occasionally. Remove the pot from the heat, cover, and let steep for 10 minutes.

3 Strain the liquid through a fine-mesh strainer or cheesecloth; do not press or squeeze the katsuobushi as this will make your dashi cloudy and not taste as nice. Spread the used katsuobishi out on a paper towel to dry, then freeze with the kombu to use in a second dashi at another time, or use it to make furikake rice seasoning (see Notes). Use the dashi stock immediately. You can store the dashi stock in the refrigerator for up to 3 days, or freeze it in ice cube trays and store in a freezer bag until needed.

NOTES Dashi can be made with kombu and katsuobushi, niboshi (baby sardines), and dried shiitake mushrooms. If you'd like to omit the fish from your dashi stock, simply use a larger piece of kombu on its own, or add in the liquid from the rehydrated wakame seaweed if you're making miso soup, or soak dried shiitake and use that liquid as well.

Instead of throwing away the used kombu and katsuoboshi after making dashi stock, you can turn it into a seasoning sprinkle for rice called furikake. Cut the used kombu into tiny pieces and crumble the katsuobushi. Toast 1 tablespoon sesame seeds in a medium pan over medium-low heat, then add in the kombu and katsuobushi bits. Reduce the heat to low and stir in 2 teaspoons soy sauce and 2 teaspoons mirin. Cook until all liquid has evaporated, about 10 minutes. Spread the mixture onto a baking sheet in a single layer and let dry fully. Crumble the mixture more and add in crumbled roasted dried seaweed. If you'd like the furikake seasoning finer, pulse in a food processor. Store in a plastic bag or small airtight container. Sprinkle over servings of plain white rice or mix with rice for Onigiri (page 62).

Another way to use the kombu from a pot of dashi in particular is to make a flavor-concentrated side dish called tsukudani that goes great with plain rice. Save up enough used kombu in an airtight container in the freezer to make 1 cup when chopped. Place in a medium pot and cover with water. Stir in 2 tablespoons sake, 1 tablespoon soy sauce, 1 tablespoon mirin, and 2 teaspoons sugar. Bring to a boil, reduce the heat to low, and simmer until the liquid is almost all gone and the kombu is tender, about 15 minutes. Add more water and simmer longer if the kombu isn't at your desired texture. Remove from the heat and toss with 1 tablespoon toasted white sesame seeds, if desired. Use on top of rice, in a bento, or even in Onigiri (page 62).

FOOD FACTS Miso paste's main ingredient is fermented soy beans, and depending on how long the mixture is fermented you get different types of miso paste. White or shiro miso is fermented for a shorter time so has a lighter flavor, whereas red or aka miso is more robust because it is fermented longer. Awase miso is a combination of the two. Miso soup can also be made with different ingredients—not only seaweed and tofu—depending on season, region, and personal taste. Oftentimes minced green onion is added, or mushrooms, seafood, carrots, daikon, or other vegetables. Simmer any ingredients that need to be cooked in the dashi before adding the miso. In *Harukana Receive*, we see the Okinawan inamuruchi, meaning "like wild boar," which is a miso with pork, konnyaku, mushroom, and fish cake.

Tonjiru, as seen in many anime including *Clean Freak! Aoyama-kun* and *Kuma Miko: Girl Meets Bear*, is another type of miso soup that is also made with pork, and can include vegetables such as carrot, daikon, burdock, taro, and more.

THIS FOOD ALSO APPEARS IN . . .

- *A Lull in the Sea*
- *Haven't You Heard? I'm Sakamoto*
- *Yuki Yuna Is a Hero*
- *The Demon Girl Next Door*
- *Is This a Zombie?*
- *Harukana Receive*
- *Tari Tari*
- *Sound of the Sky*
- *The Helpful Fox Senko-san*
- *Hello!! Kinmoza!*

THE SECRET WORLD OF ARRIETTY

CREAM STEW

White Stew with Vegetables

SERVES 4 This creamy broth mixed with tiny bits of broccoli and carrots, pilfered from the huge kitchen above the floorboards, is served in minuscule bowls as a comforting and hearty meal to a (literally) small family. Four-inch-tall Arrietty is a Borrower, a tiny being who "borrows" items from Human Beans (humans) to survive and lives alongside them undetected. Well, mostly undetected. While obtaining a sugar cube and a tissue, Arrietty is discovered by Sho, a twelve-year-old boy who is ill with a heart condition, and the two eventually become secret friends.

- **1 teaspoon salt, plus more for seasoning**
- **1 cup broccoli florets, cut into bite-size pieces**
- **1 tablespoon vegetable or canola oil**
- **¼ pound boneless, skinless chicken breasts or thighs, cut into bite-size pieces**
- **White pepper**
- **½ large onion, roughly chopped**
- **1 large carrot, peeled and cut into bite-size pieces**
- **1 medium potato, peeled and cut into bite-size pieces**
- **2 cups vegetable or chicken broth**
- **1 bay leaf**
- **2 tablespoons unsalted butter**
- **2 tablespoons all-purpose flour**
- **1½ cup milk, at room temperature**

1 In a large pot over high heat, bring 3 cups of water plus 1 teaspoon of salt to a boil. In the meantime, fill a large bowl halfway with cold water and add several ice cubes to make an ice bath. Add the broccoli to the boiling water and cook for 3 minutes, or until the broccoli is bright green and only slightly tender. Drain the hot cooking water and place the broccoli in the ice bath. Once the broccoli is cold, strain it and let it sit in the strainer in the sink until needed.

2 Heat the oil in a large pot over medium heat and stir in the chicken pieces with a pinch each of salt and pepper. Sauté until lightly cooked on all sides, 3 to 4 minutes, then stir in the onion and carrot and cook for another minute. Stir in the potato, then pour in the broth; if the broth doesn't cover the vegetables, add enough water to compensate. Lay the bay leaf on top and bring to a boil. Cover the pot with a lid, reduce the heat to low, and simmer for 12 minutes, or until the carrots are tender. Skim off any foam as needed.

3 While the stew is simmering, melt the butter in a medium pot over low heat. Add the flour and stir constantly until fully incorporated, about 6 minutes. Remove the pot from the heat and quickly whisk in a quarter of the milk until smooth. Return the pot to low heat and gradually whisk in the remaining milk until the sauce is smooth and thickened.

4 Remove the bay leaf from the stew and pour in the milk and flour mixture. Stir gently to incorporate, being careful not to break the vegetables. Add the broccoli and stir gently again. Season with salt and pepper.

NOTE Cream stew is typically made with chicken as the meat, but pork and shrimp are sometimes used instead. Arrietty's stew seems to be vegetarian, which is also a great option. You could even cut the carrots into shapes, like hearts in *Show By Rock!!* and stars in *March Comes in Like a Lion*. Other ingredients for cream stew can include cauliflower, corn, green beans, peas, kabocha, and mushrooms. Cream stew is also shown served over rice in *March Comes in Like a Lion*, and the more adventurous could even try the unique version with spaghetti noodles, asparagus, pork, and cheese from *Laid-Back Camp*.

FOOD FACTS Cream stew, similar to what it is today in Japan, was created after World War II for schoolchildren as a way to increase their milk intake and give them something hearty to eat to boost their health and energy. As those children grew up, making cream stew at home became more common, and since the late 1960s it has been a staple of Japanese comfort food.

THIS FOOD ALSO APPEARS IN . . .

- *Pokémon*
- *Trigun*
- *Log Horizon*
- *Fate/kaleid liner Prisma Illya*
- *Cowboy Bebop*
- *5 Centimeters Per Second*
- *Garo: The Animation*
- *Tsubasa RESERVoir CHRoNiCLE*
- *Space Brothers*
- *Is the Order a Rabbit?*
- *Today's Menu for the Emiya Family*
- *Polar Bear Café*
- *Accel World*
- *Haganai: I Don't Have Many Friends*
- *Show By Rock!!*
- *March Comes in Like a Lion*

SHIELD
桜

CARDCAPTOR SAKURA

TAMAGOYAKI

Rolled Egg Omelet

SERVES 2 With a lot of practice and determination—between fighting battles, collecting Clow cards, and being an elementary school student—magical girl Sakura Kinomoto has finally mastered making tasty tamagoyaki. Now, like her father and brother, she can prepare delicious bento for those she loves.

1 tablespoon canola or vegetable oil, plus more as needed
3 large eggs
1 tablespoon Dashi Stock (page 56) or 1/2 teaspoon dashi granules with 1 tablespoon water
1 tablespoon mirin
1 1/2 teaspoons sugar
1/2 teaspoon usukuchi (light-colored) soy sauce

1 Heat the oil in a medium pan over medium-low heat and use a folded paper towel to wipe the oil around the pan. In a glass measuring cup, combine the eggs, dashi or water, mirin, sugar, usukuchi soy sauce. Whisk well to break up the eggs completely.

2 Once the pan is hot, pour a third of the egg mixture into the pan and tilt the pan to spread the mixture around so it covers the bottom completely. When the bottom of the egg is set but the top is still slightly runny, use a spatula or two to carefully roll the egg up starting from one side, creating a log shape. Slide the log to the side of the pan that you started on and re-oil the pan. Pour another third of the egg mixture into the pan, lifting the log slightly to let some of the liquid slide underneath. When the bottom of the new layer of egg is set and the top is jiggly, roll the log carefully up and over to the opposite side of the pan again, then slide it back. Repeat this process with the remaining egg mixture. Once all of the egg mixture is used up, turn the tamagoyaki seam side down for 15 seconds to set it.

3 Remove the pan from the heat and gently slide the egg roll onto a cutting board. If you'd like to shape the tamagoyaki into more of a rectangle, lay a sheet of plastic wrap over it, then lay a sushi mat on top, pressing it gently into shape around the tamagoyaki. Let the tamagoyaki sit until cool enough to handle, then slice across widthwise into 3/4-inch- to 1-inch-wide segments.

NOTE Tamagoyaki is pretty versatile and can be made with various ingredients, such as grated carrots, corn, shredded crab meat, roasted nori, or spinach between the layers, or even cheese at the center, like in *Gourmet Girl Graffiti*.

TAMAGO NIGIRI

Chances are, you've seen or eaten tamago nigiri—sushi with a slice of egg omelet on top—at a sushi restaurant (or seen it in *Servamp* or other anime).

Whip up a batch of sushi rice (see page 52) and 1 recipe of tamagoyaki. Let the tamagoyaki cool to room temperature, then slice it in half widthwise. Cut off the rounded sides and continue to cut into 1/4-inch-wide slices. Wet your hands and form a palm-size portion of sushi rice into a compact oblong shape (plastic wrap can make this easier). Lay a slice of egg on top, then wrap the whole thing with a long strip of dried nori seaweed about 1/4 inch wide, snipping off the excess after wrapping. Repeat with the rest of the rice and tamago slices.

ANIME FACTS *Cardcaptor Sakura* is one of the many memorable anime and manga from the all-woman manga group CLAMP. Other CLAMP stories include *RG Veda, X/1999, xxxHolic, Magic Knight Rayearth, Tokyo Babylon, Chobits, Miyuki-chan in Wonderland, Angelic Layer,* and many more.

THIS FOOD ALSO APPEARS IN . . .

- *Soul Eater NOT!*
- *Gourmet Girl Graffiti*
- *Death Parade*
- *Okko's Inn*
- *Fate/stay night: Heaven's Feel*
- *School Rumble*
- *Is This a Zombie?*
- *Dusk Maiden of Amnesia*
- *Re-Kan!*
- *Sailor Moon*

FRUITS BASKET

ONIGIRI

Rice Balls

SERVES 2 In the game of Fruits Basket, where players are dubbed different fruits and called to join the "basket" at different times, someone dubbed an onigiri has no place. Tohru Honda was called an onigiri when she was little and has always felt like she doesn't belong. She doesn't let this get her down, though, and remains kind and tries her best, no matter what life throws at her. As she explains, we're all like onigiri and often can't recognize our own value; we see the special umeboshi on the backs of others but not on ourselves. But it's there! You just need to turn around and look.

Salt
2 cups cooked Rice (see page 52)
Filling of your choice (see Notes)
2 (2 x 5-inch) strips dried nori seaweed (optional)

1 Pour 2 tablespoons of water into a small bowl to dip your fingers in as you work so that the rice doesn't stick to you. Line another small bowl with a large sheet of plastic wrap, flick a bit of water onto it, and sprinkle on a dash of salt (the salt adds flavor and also acts to preserve the rice). Scoop ½ cup of cooked rice into the plastic-lined bowl, then make a well in the center for 1 tablespoon of filling. Fold the edges of the rice over to cover the filling, then gather up the edges of the plastic wrap and lift it out of the bowl, twisting the plastic closed while pushing out the air. With the rice in the plastic, press and shape it into a compact, rounded triangle with no filling showing. Add little bits of rice to cover up any exposed filling if necessary. The triangle is a common and very recognizable onigiri shape, but cylinders and rounds are also common, as they can often fit in a bento box more easily; you may need to make them half-size, though.

2 Unwrap the onigiri and lay it on a plate. Repeat the process with the rest of the rice. If you decide to add the nori strips, you can put them on now; or, if you'll be eating the onigiri later, you can keep the nori separate so that it doesn't absorb moisture and become limp. To add the nori, fold a nori strip around one side of the onigiri, often the bottom. If you'd like to wrap a larger or longer piece of nori around the onigiri so that the ends overlap, crush a rice grain between your fingers and use it to "glue" the ends together.

NOTES The name *onigiri* comes from the Japanese word *nigiru*, which means "to form" or "press into shape." Tohru makes onigiri with many different fillings, including umeboshi (salty pickled plum) and chives (or some say leeks!). Other filling ideas are flaked Shiozake (page 14), canned tuna or shredded chicken with mayonnaise, Karaage (page 66), shrimp tempura dipped in a little tentsuyu (page 15), kinpira gobo (page 71), shiokombu (salted kelp), kimchi, seasoned meat, salmon roe . . . You can put so many things into an onigiri! You can also forgo a filling and simply mix the rice with edamame, corn, tenkasu tempura bits, kinpira, or furikake, then shape it. Tohru decorates her onigiri with shapes cut from seaweed sheets.

If you'd like to prepare some easy garlic chives for onigiri filling, chop the ends off of a small bundle—if you can't find them, use regular chives plus ½ teaspoon of minced garlic—and cut into 1-inch pieces. Heat 1 teaspoon of canola or vegetable oil in a small pan over medium heat and toss the chives to coat. Add a pinch of salt and stir in a teaspoon of soy sauce if desired, and cook until the chives are just softened, stirring often. Let cool for a few minutes before using.

ANIME FACTS Between the translations of the *Fruits Basket* manga and both anime adaptations, there is a discrepancy on what Yuki is growing in his garden—is it leeks or chives? And which one does Kyo hate? The earlier English translations stated leeks, which is *negi* in Japanese, but in actuality the Japanese word used is *nira*, which is garlic chives, also known as Chinese chives, and the newer translations reflect this. Both leeks and chives are in the *allium* genus of onions and garlics and thus have very strong flavors, but they do taste different.

In *One Piece*, three of Roronoa Zoro's santoryu (triple sword) attacks are plays on onigiri. The words *oni* and *kiri* mean "ogre" or "demon" and "to cut" or "slash," respectively, which is one attack style, "ogre cutting." The next attack is *yaki oni kiri*, which is referencing a grilled onigiri, and becomes "burning ogre cutter" in translation. The third attack is a phonetic play on words with *enbima yonezu oni kiri*, which becomes ebi and mayonezu (shrimp mayonnaise) onigiri. The attack itself is akin to "charming sleepless night ogre cutter."

Onigiri are sometimes called rice balls in anime, manga, and video games, but nothing beats the infamous 4Kids Entertainment translation change of calling them jelly-filled doughnuts!

THIS FOOD ALSO APPEARS IN . . .

- *Spirited Away*
- *Urusei Yatsura*
- *Shirobako*
- *Shugo Chara!! Doki*
- *Higurashi When They Cry*
- *Demon Slayer: Kimetsu no Yaiba*
- *The Eccentric Family*
- *Chihayafuru*
- *One-Punch Man*
- *Natsume's Book of Friends*
- *The Story of Saiunkoku*
- *Hakuoki: Dawn of the Shinsengumi*
- *Kids on the Slope*
- *Sengoku Collection*
- *Cute High Earth Defense Club LOVE!*

KIMI NI TODOKE: FROM ME TO YOU

ASPARA BACON

Asparagus Wrapped in Bacon

SERVES 2 Perfect for a bento to share with friends.

6 asparagus stalks
1 tablespoon vegetable or canola oil
3 strips bacon, cut in half
Salt and freshly ground black pepper

1 Bring enough water to cover the asparagus to boil in a medium pot. Cut the hard ends off the asparagus, about 1 inch depending on the size of the stalks, and use a peeler to remove any hard skin. Cut each asparagus into 3 equal segments. Prepare an ice bath of cold water with several ice cubes in a medium bowl. Drop the cut asparagus into the pot of boiling water and cook for 2 minutes, until they are a beautiful bright green. Immediately strain the asparagus and place them in the ice bath. Remove the asparagus once they are cooled and pat dry with paper towels.

2 Heat the oil in a large pan over medium-low heat. Wrap 3 asparagus segments in one of the bacon halves and secure with a toothpick. Repeat with the remaining asparagus segments and bacon strips. Once the pan is hot, place the wraps in the pan and cook for 8 minutes, turning to brown all sides. Turn off the heat and place the aspara bacon on a paper towel to remove excess bacon grease. Season with salt and pepper and serve as part of a meal or use in bento.

FOOD FACTS Aspara bacon is seen often in anime, usually in bento (page 78), and sometimes as a side dish to a larger meal. In *Hanasaku Iroha*, we see Minko putting aspara bacon on skewers. This is a type of kushiyaki, or skewered and grilled food that you can sometimes find at yakitori restaurants.

Of course, since we're not sure if she grilled or fried her aspara bacon, they could also be kushiage, which means "skewered and fried." You could even bake them; line the skewers or individual wraps on a wire cooling rack set over a foil-lined baking sheet and bake at 350°F for 15 to 20 minutes.

Other wraps similar to aspara bacon seen in anime are green beans, okra, or carrot strips wrapped in thin beef or pork belly slices.

CULTURE FACTS *Asupara behkon maki kei otoko*, meaning "asparagus bacon roll–men," is a term sometimes used by women in Japan to describe men who pretend to be outwardly self-assured and macho but are actually unassertive or indifferent in relationships, or have low self-confidence at their center. This idea is a combination of two other terms used in Japan: "carnivore men" and "herbivore men."

THIS FOOD ALSO APPEARS IN . . .

- *Tsukigakirei*
- *Free! Eternal Summer*
- *Blood-C*
- *One Week Friends*
- *Log Horizon*
- *Qualidea Code*
- *AKB0048*
- *BanG Dream!*
- *Hundred*
- *Aikatsu!*
- *Haruchika*
- *Gate*
- *K-On!*

SHIROBAKO

KARAAGE

Deep-Fried Chicken Pieces

SERVES 3 Creating anime is an intense and in-depth process that depends on dedicated and hardworking teams of people. Production assistant Aoi Miyamori works at the lively Musashino Animation studio and learns the ins and outs of the industry amid a colorful crew of coworkers, each with their own strengths and difficulties. Through deadlines and delays, their dedication and passion—as well as the large amounts of karaage the animation studio president makes—help them produce work that they can be proud of.

1 pound boneless chicken thighs, cut into bite-size pieces

2 tablespoons soy sauce

1 tablespoon sake

¼ teaspoon finely grated fresh ginger

Vegetable or canola oil, for frying

2 tablespoons potato starch (also called katakuriko)

2 tablespoons cake flour

FOR SERVING

Lemon wedges (optional)

Oroshi (finely grated daikon, optional)

1 Place the chicken pieces in a large bowl and coat with the soy sauce, sake, and ginger, making sure the marinade is evenly distributed. Cover the bowl with plastic wrap and place in the refrigerator for 30 minutes to 1 hour, depending on how flavorful you'd like your chicken.

2 Set a wire cooling rack, with a baking sheet or foil underneath, near your stove. Heat 1½ inches of oil in a large pan to 340°F. Remove the chicken from the refrigerator. Sift the potato starch and cake flour in a shallow dish and coat each piece of chicken separately with starch, squeezing each piece gently to compact it. Place the coated chicken pieces on another plate until the oil is ready.

3 Lower 4 to 5 pieces of chicken into the oil at a time, depending on the size of your pan, making sure not to overcrowd the oil. Cook the chicken on both sides until a deep golden brown, 3 to 4 minutes total. Remove with tongs or a slotted spoon or strainer onto the cooling rack. Repeat the cooking process in batches until all of the chicken is cooked. Keep your eye on the temperature and scoop away any browned bits in the oil as you go along. Serve immediately or use in a bento. Serve with lemon wedges and/or oroshi.

FOOD FACTS Traditionally, chicken that was marinated before being coated in katakuriko and deep-fried was called tatsutaage, after the Tatsuta Gawa river and its beautiful golden foliage in autumn. What was called chicken karaage was not marinated but simply coated in flour, or a mixture of flour and katakuriko, and then deep-fried. Nowadays it's pretty much all called karaage, which is actually just the term for coating meat with flour or starch and then frying it. This type of food is so often made with chicken, though, that now when someone says karaage, they mean the chicken kind.

ANIME FACT Shirobako means "white box" and refers to the VHS cassette tapes in white boxes that the animation production team would receive before the anime officially aired. VHS tapes, of course, are no longer used, but the term shirobako remains for the final digital files more often used today, and the CD version seen in *Shirobako*.

THIS FOOD ALSO APPEARS IN . . .

- *Sanrio Boys*
- *Run with the Wind*
- *Cardcaptor Sakura*
- *Glasslip*
- *Fresh Pretty Cure!*
- *True Cooking Master Boy*
- *Okojo-san's Happy Apartment*
- *Diabolik Lovers II: More, Blood*
- *Masamune-kun's Revenge*
- *Slow Start*
- *March Comes in Like a Lion*
- *IDOLiSH7*
- *My First Girlfriend Is a Gal*
- *Haikyuu!!*
- *Today's Menu for the Emiya Family*
- *The Pet Girl of Sakurasou*

STAEDTLER
Mars Lumograph
STAEDTLER

SWEETNESS & LIGHTNING

GYOZA

Savory Filled Dumplings

MAKES 30 TO 35 DUMPLINGS Kohei Inuzuka is doing his best to raise his daughter, Tsumugi, after the passing of his wife, but preparing nourishing and consistent meals, like she used to make, is proving a problem as he usually resorts to takeout and premade foods. That is, until he and Tsumugi meet lonely Kotori, who is the daughter of a popular and often absent chef, and a student at the same school in which Inuzuka teaches. They start meeting at Kotori's small family restaurant so that they can all learn to cook sustaining and meaningful meals together, one such meal being warm gyoza, soft and crispy at once.

FOR THE FILLING

½ head Napa cabbage or ¼ head Napa and ¼ head round cabbage

¾ teaspoon salt

¼ pound ground pork

¼ cup Chinese chives, or 1 tablespoon minced garlic and 3 tablespoons chives

1 leek, white and pale green parts minced

1 green onion, white and pale green parts minced

1 tablespoon sake

1 tablespoon soy sauce

2 teaspoons sesame oil

2 teaspoons cornstarch

1 teaspoon grated fresh ginger

¼ teaspoon freshly ground black pepper

FOR THE WRAPPERS

½ cup all-purpose flour, plus more for dusting

1 tablespoon sesame oil

5 tablespoons hot water

Pinch of salt

Cornstarch, for dusting

1 tablespoon vegetable oil

1 Core and mince the cabbage, place in a bowl, and toss with ½ teaspoon of salt. Let sit for 10 minutes, then drain, rinse, and squeeze dry in a paper towel. Combine the cabbage with the remaining ¼ teaspoon salt, ground pork, chives, leeks, green onions, sake, soy sauce, sesame oil, cornstarch, ginger, and black pepper in a large bowl. Mix with your hands until sticky and fully incorporated. Cover the bowl with plastic wrap and chill in the refrigerator for 1 hour.

2 Meanwhile, make the wrappers: Stir together the flour, sesame oil, hot water, and salt until combined. Transfer the dough to a lightly floured surface. Knead at least 100 times—pushing the heel of your hand into the dough, pushing up, folding the dough over, and repeating—until smooth. Shape into a log, wrap in plastic, and rest on the counter for 30 minutes.

3 Divide the dough in half to be more manageable and work with one half at a time, keeping the other half under the plastic wrap. On a flat surface lightly dusted with cornstarch, roll the dough segment out very flat, to about 1/16 inch. Use a 4-inch-round cookie cutter, or a lid or bowl of similar size to cut 30 to 35 circles from the dough, or as many as you can. Stack the disks under plastic wrap with a bit of cornstarch in between each disk. Repeat with the remaining piece of dough, rerolling any excess dough until all is used. (Keep a little dough to the side if you'd like to form bows like Tsumugi puts on the gyoza she makes in the show.)

4 To form the gyoza, have a bowl of water nearby. Take a dough disk and place a scant tablespoon of filling in the center. Use your finger to smear a bit of water on one edge, then fold the opposite edge to meet it. Pleat and press one edge, causing the seam to curve like a crescent. Transfer to a baking sheet and cover with plastic wrap while you repeat the process until all of the disks are filled. (If you're adding Tsumugi's tiny dough bows, press them on now with a little water.)

5 Spread the oil in a large pan over medium heat. Add the gyoza, keeping their pleated seams up, and cook until the bottoms are crispy and browned. Pour in ¼ cup water and cover to steam until the water has mostly evaporated. Remove the lid and continue cooking to evaporate the water compltetely and make sure the bottoms are very crispy and browned, about 12 to 15 minutes. If you'd like to try to flip the gyoza onto a plate like Kohei does, turn off the heat, make sure none of the gyoza are sticking to the pan, and place a large plate upside down over the pan. Using potholders if needed, invert the pan and plate so that the gyoza fall onto the plate crispy bottoms up; this is the typical way to serve them.

NOTE If you'd like to make a quick dipping sauce, simply combine 1 to 2 tablespoons rice vinegar, according to your taste, with 2 tablespoons soy sauce. Stir in a few drops of spicy la-yu (sometimes called rayu) oil, if desired.

FOOD FACTS The name *gyoza* is derived from the Chinese word *jiaozi*, China being the origin of these tasty morsels. They are also sometimes referred to as potstickers or dumplings. Japanese gyoza are often smaller than their Chinese counterparts and made with thinner dough. There are various ways to prepare gyoza; this recipe is for the yaki, or fried, version. *Sweetness & Lightning* shows them boiled in a light broth known as sui gyoza, as well as stuffing the filling into chicken wings, called teba gyoza—which is also seen in *Food Wars!*. Another way to cook them is by deep-frying, known as age gyoza.

THIS FOOD ALSO APPEARS IN . . .

- *Shirobako*
- *Mix: Meisei Story*
- *Hakata Tonkotsu Ramens*
- *THE IDOL-M@STER: SideM*
- *ClassicaLoid*
- *Kuromukuro*
- *The Pet Girl of Sakurasou*
- *Beyond the Boundary*
- *Hozuki's Coolheadedness*
- *Kakuriyo: Bed & Breakfast for Spirits*
- *Maison Ikkoku*
- *True Cooking Master Boy*
- *Ms. Koizumi Loves Ramen Noodles*
- *Cardcaptor Sakura: Clear Card*

CHOBITS

KINPIRA GOBO

Sautéed and Simmered Burdock Root

SERVES 4 After receiving a rejection letter from the university he applied to, young farmer Hideki Motosuwa decides to leave his rural life and move to the city for college prep school. He's wowed by the technological advancements of city life, especially the persocom personal robot companions (which resemble beautiful girls) that almost everyone seems to have. While bemoaning his lack of girlfriend and persocom, Hideki stumbles upon an abandoned persocom in the trash. He takes the robot home, figures out how to activate it after much unfortunate groping, and is then discovered with the unclothed robot girl on top of him by his pretty landlady, who was only stopping by to give him a container of kinpira gobo.

- **1/2 teaspoon rice vinegar**
- **1 burdock root**
- **1 tablespoon sesame oil**
- **1 large carrot**
- **1 tablespoon soy sauce**
- **1 tablespoon sake**
- **1 tablespoon mirin**
- **2 teaspoons sugar**
- **1/4 cup Dashi Stock (page 56)**
- **2 teaspoons white sesame seeds**

1 Fill a medium bowl half full with cold water and stir in the vinegar. Under cold running water, scrub the burdock root well, then scrape the skin away with the back of a knife. Place the root on a cutting board and cut into 2-inch segments, then cut those segments lengthwise into 1/8-inch slices. Stack the slices a few at a time and cut into matchsticks 2 inches long. Place the matchsticks into the bowl of cold water as you go, letting them soak for 5 minutes.

2 Heat the sesame oil in a large pot over medium-high heat. Drain the cut burdock and pat dry with paper towels. Place in the hot pot, toss to coat with the oil, and cook for 2 minutes. Add the carrots to the pot with the burdock and stir, cooking for 3 minutes. Stir in the soy sauce, sake, mirin, and sugar and cook for another minute. Pour in the dashi and reduce the heat to medium. Simmer, stirring occasionally, until the liquid is mostly absorbed or evaporated, about 10 minutes.

3 Remove the pot from the heat and fold in the sesame seeds. Scoop into serving dishes and serve at room temperature, or store in an airtight container in the refrigerator overnight for the flavors to meld more.

NOTES If you're unable to find burdock root, you can substitute salsify root, or even parsnips. They are not the same, but will do in a pinch.

Kinpira gobo is often a side dish for a meal or used in bento, but you can make a donburi with it like in *Tari Tari*—rice topped with kinpira gobo plus a shiozake fillet (see page 14; you can leave off the salmon and it'll still be a donburi). Kinpira is also great as an onigiri filling (see page 62) or used in kakiage tempura (page 15).

FOOD FACTS Burdock root has been used for its health benefits for thousands of years all over the world, but Japan is unique in its consumption of the root in common dishes. Aside from kinpira gobo, burdock root is used in kakiage tempura, tonjiru miso soup, pounded tataki gobo, takikomi gohan, various nimono, and many other recipes.

ANIME FACTS *Gobo* is the Japanese name for burdock root. In *Dragon Ball* canon, Goku's dad's name is Bardock for burdock, and Goku's Saiyan name is Kakarot for carrot . . . put them together, and you've got this common Japanese side dish, kinpira gobo!

THIS FOOD ALSO APPEARS IN . . .

- *Ben-To*
- *Tari Tari*
- *Death Parade*
- *Orange*
- *A Lull in the Sea*
- *Urusei Yatsura*
- *Your Name*
- *Space Brothers*
- *Blood Lad*
- *Slow Start*
- *Persona 4: The Animation*
- *Wedding Peach DX*
- *Convenience Store Boy Friends*
- *Re-Kan!*
- *Monthly Girls' Nozaki-Kun*
- *Gourmet Girl Graffiti*
- *K-On!*
- *Food Wars!*
- *Encouragement of Climb*

BARAKAMON

PICKLED DAIKON

Marinated Daikon White Radish

SERVES 4 Having hit a creative wall—and someone's nose—professional Japanese calligrapher Seishu Handa is forced to take a break from city life and go to Fukue Island, where life moves at a slower pace. There he meets the energetic six-year-old Naru Kotoishi and her kind grandfather, who gifts Handa-kun with his special daikon radish pickles called konomon. Handa-kun isn't very enthusiastic about the gift at first, but once he tastes it, he's hooked.

10 ounces daikon radish
¼ cup sugar
1 tablespoon unseasoned rice vinegar
1 tablespoon usukuchi (light-colored soy sauce)
1 tablespoon sake
½ small dried red chile pepper, seeds removed, chopped (optional)

1 Peel and slice the daikon into ⅛-inch-thick discs and cut the discs in half. Lay the half circles in a single layer on a large baking sheet lined with paper towels, then cover with another layer of paper towels. Let sit on the counter for 3 days to dry.

2 In a small pot over medium-low heat, combine the sugar, vinegar, usukuchi, and sake. Cook until the sugar is dissolved, stirring occasionally, then remove from the heat to cool.

3 Place the daikon pieces in a large freezer bag and pour the liquid over them. If you'd like to add some spice, sprinkle in the chile pepper. Close the bag and massage the daikon to coat well with the marinade. Place the bag in the refrigerator for 2 days. To serve, remove the daikon pickles from the marinade and eat as a side dish to a meal or in a bento.

NOTES Grandpa Kotoishi's konomon are a type of tsukemono, or "pickled thing," and are compared to hari hari zuke, or pickled dried daikon, in the manga. The recipe above doesn't dry the daikon pieces for as long as Grandpa does—until they're small and ruffle-y—but you can dry them longer if you'd like. Grandpa also quarters his daikon slices so they become very small when dried.

A common daikon tsukemono is the vibrantly yellow takuan. It's made using dried whole daikon in rice bran, sometimes with the addition of persimmon peels, and is left to ferment for several months. If you'd like the pickles from the recipe above to be yellow, add in several threads of saffron or ¼ teaspoon of ground turmeric.

QUICK DAIKON PICKLES

Peel 10 ounces daikon and cut into ⅛-inch slices. Toss the slices with 1 teaspoon salt in a medium bowl, cover with plastic, and sit a small, weighted plate on top for 1 hour to draw out the moisture and bitterness. Drain and quickly rinse the daikon slices under cold water, squeeze gently, and pat dry with paper towels. Combine ¼ cup unseasoned rice vinegar and 2 tablespoons sugar in a large freezer bag and add the daikon. Press out the air, seal the bag, and massage to coat the slices completely. Place the bag in the refrigerator for at least 1 hour—the longer the marinating time, the stronger the flavor. Add more sugar to taste, if you'd like, and red pepper flakes for spice.

FOOD FACTS Both white and yellow pickled daikon are seen in anime in little dishes on the side of a meal, often with cucumber pickles (see page 81). Tsukemono are considered palate-cleansers, eaten in between bites or between dishes, or eaten at the end of the meal to aid in digestion. They are referred to as hashi yasume, which means "chopstick rest."

ANIME FACTS Barakamon means "a cheerful person," or denotes a person with a lot of energy in the native dialect of the Goto Islands, of which Fukue Island, where *Barakamon* takes place, is a part. Little Naru is at first glance the main energetic and cheerful character, loving her island home and viewing all things with wonder. Over time that attitude of finding seemingly everyday sights and occurrences interesting and beautiful rubs off on Handa-kun and helps him in his art and character growth. He certainly gets energetic about konomon!

THIS FOOD ALSO APPEARS IN . . .

- *Penguindrum*
- *Onihei*
- *K-On!*
- *March Comes in Like a Lion*
- *Restaurant to Another World*
- *A Lull in the Sea*
- *THE IDOL-M@STER*
- *Natsume's Book of Friends*
- *Kuma Miko: Girl Meets Bear*
- *Hanasaku Iroha: Blossoms for Tomorrow*
- *Kamisama Kiss*

FUTURE DIARY

POTATO SALAD

SERVES 4 TO 6 Is it his mom's home cooking that self-proclaimed weakling Yukiteru Amano is eating? He's missed her during these terrifying times of god-games, future-predicting cell phone diaries, and pursuit by potential murderers. After commenting on the large amount of potato salad, Yukiteru's mother informs him that she's not the one who made the meal; rather, it was his friend Yuno Gasai. Yukiteru trembles, imagining that she's still there, afraid that she might be an enemy, and terrified even more by her obsessive and insanely intense love for him.

- **1/4 English cucumber, sliced into 1/16-inch-thick disks**
- **1/2 large carrot, sliced into thin strips**
- **1/4 large onion, diced**
- **1/2 teaspoon salt, plus more for seasoning**
- **2 cups diced potatoes (about 2 medium potatoes)**
- **1 large egg**
- **2 tablespoons Kewpie mayonnaise**
- **1 1/2 teaspoons rice vinegar**
- **1/2 teaspoon sugar**
- **1 thick slice deli ham, cut into bite-size strips**

1 Place the sliced cucumber, carrot, and onion in a medium bowl, toss with 1/2 teaspoon salt, and set aside until needed.

2 Fill a small bowl with cold water and add a few ice cubes to create an ice bath. Place the potatoes in a large pot over high heat and cover with water. Once the water starts boiling, add the egg and cook for 9 minutes. Transfer the egg to the ice bath to cool. Cook the potatoes for another 5 minutes, or until tender. Drain the water from the pot but keep the potatoes in, reducing the heat to low. Stir the potatoes around occasionally to help any excess water to evaporate. Transfer the potatoes to a large bowl.

3 Peel and dice the egg. Add the mayonnaise, vinegar, and sugar to the potatoes and toss to coat. Smash the potatoes with the back of a spoon or a potato masher, keeping the mixture chunky.

4 Drain the liquid from the cucumber mixture and gently squeeze the pieces, then pat them dry with paper towels. Fold the cucumber mixture into the potato mixture, along with the diced egg and ham pieces, until evenly distributed. Taste the potato salad and adjust the salt, sugar, or vinegar as needed.

FOOD FACTS Japanese potato salad is great as a side dish to a meal, but is also wonderful in bento (page 78). You'll often see it in anime formed into a ball and placed in a little paper cup or lettuce leaf like in *The Disappearance of Nagato Yuki-chan* or *Kannagi: Crazy Shrine Maidens*. Other common ingredients include corn, cooked shrimp, peas, and cooked green beans. In *Gourmet Girl Graffiti*, Kirin even adds sliced chikuwa, which is a type of kamaboko fish cake.

Another popular way to eat potatoes as a side dish is kofuki imo, which means "powdered potatoes." Simply peel and cube a potato and boil it until just tender, drain the water, and continue to cook, shaking the pan every so often, until the moisture evaporates and the potato chunks become powdery-looking, adding salt and other seasonings as desired. Steamed potatoes are also popular, at home and at festivals, especially with butter (see page 96).

CULTURE FACTS Potatoes, originating in the Americas, were introduced to Japan by Dutch traders in the late 1500s and early 1600s, but large-scale cultivation of potatoes didn't start until the late 1800s in Hokkaido. The name *jagaimo* was originally *jagatora imo*; *imo* for "tuber" and *jagatora* (shortened later to *jaga*) for Jakarta, Indonesia, where the port that the traders came through with the potatoes was located. The most famous variety of potato in Japan is the danshaku, meaning "baron," named for Baron Ryukichi Kawata, who introduced the variety in the early 1900s. Potatoes were a lifesaving food in post–World War II Japan when shortages of rice and other staple foods were an issue.

THIS FOOD ALSO APPEARS IN . . .

- *Digimon Adventure tri. 2: Determination*
- *Kannagi: Crazy Shrine Maidens*
- *Bunny Drop*
- *Gourmet Girl Graffiti*
- *Fresh Pretty Cure!*
- *Charlotte*
- *Kill la Kill*
- *Log Horizon*
- *Haruchika*
- *Wakakozake*
- *Yuri Bear Storm*
- *Luck & Logic*
- *Kuroko's Basketball*
- *Blue Spring Ride*
- *World Trigger*

RUN
RUN
squirrel
食べられる!
うずらも
へんしん
おどる
うさぎ

BENTO

Bento can be found all over anime, most often as school lunches, but also on long train rides, at picnics, and at work.

These meals can be made lovingly at home or bought quickly at a konbini, or convenience store. Bento refers to a convenient, one-person meal, and also specifically to the box containing the meal.

Bento typically feature a colorful variety of food in small, separated portions, tightly packed together in a plastic, wooden, or stainless-steel box. Square *furoshiki* cloths are wrapped around the outside of homemade bento to act as a carrying bag, as well as a tablecloth while eating.

Bento often feature colorful food separators along with the colorful food. Separators can be little silicone or paper cups (like those used for muffins and cupcakes), plastic partitions (like those used with store-bought sushi), and fresh lettuce or shiso (also known as perilla) leaves.

Bento are packed tightly so the contents don't move around too much in the box, and also to get as much deliciousness into the meal as possible. Steamed broccoli and cherry tomatoes are often used to fill gaps in bento.

Oekakiben and kyaraben are two very creative and decorative styles of bento that use food to form images. The first means "picture bento" and depicts scenes, animals, and people; the second means "character bento" and depicts pop-culture characters. You can see these types of bento in *Shin Atashinchi, Orange*, *Nurse Witch Komugi R*, *School Babysitters*, *Clean Freak! Aoyama-kun, Your Name*, and many more anime.

Along with a pleasing variety of color, bento should also feature different textures of food, and be chosen based on carbohydrates, protein, and fruits and vegetables—the amounts following that order with carbohydrates taking up the largest section of bento.

Have you seen the bento rice with an umeboshi pickled plum exactly in the center? This is called hinomaru, meaning "circle of the sun," and represents the red circle on the Japanese flag that symbolizes the rising sun (Japan is known as "the land of the rising sun"). Another popular rice topping is furikake, which is a dry, crumbly, or powdery seasoning that comes in many varieties. Did you know you can make your own furikake from the leftover kombu seaweed and katsuobushi flakes used in making Dashi Stock (page 56)?

COOK ANIME BENTO OPTIONS

CARBOHYDRATES

- **Rice,** page 52
- **Chahan,** page 55
- **Onigiri,** page 62
- **Inarizushi,** page 53
- **Kappamaki,** page 81
- **Omurice,** page 40
- **Napolitan,** page 45
- **Yakisoba,** page 84
- **Korokke,** page 90
- **Potato Salad,** page 74

PROTEINS

- **Shiozake,** page 14
- **Ebi Furai,** page 18
- **Tamagoyaki,** page 61
- **Aspara Bacon,** page 65
- **Karaage,** page 66
- **Tonkatsu,** page 35
- **Hambagu,** page 49
- **Gyudon,** page 39
- **Gyoza,** page 68
- **Nikujaga,** page 24
- **Chinjou Rosu,** page 43
- **Omurice,** page 40 (for the egg)
- **Tako Sausages** (recipe follows)

VEGETABLES & FRUIT

- **Ohitashi,** page 80
- **Goma-ae,** page 80
- **Kinpira Gobo,** page 71
- **Kyuri Asazuke,** page 81
- **Pickled Daikon,** page 72
- **Kabocha Nimono,** page 24
- **Usagi Ringo** (recipe follows)
- **Nikujaga,** page 24
- **Chinjao Rosu,** page 43
- **Aspara Bacon,** page 65

USAGI RINGO

Usagi ringo, or "apple rabbits," are common in anime bento. *Usagi* means "rabbit" in Japanese, and *ringo* means "apple." These make for a refreshing addition to a meal, or as a to-go snack.

½ teaspoon salt

1 crisp red apple

1 Combine 2 tablespoons water with the salt in a small shallow dish and set aside. Remove the stem and cut the apple into quarters. Cut the apple core from each quarter, then cut each quarter in half, creating 8 wedges.

2 Working with one wedge at a time, slice a shallow inverted V in the skin, ¾ inch down from one end, making the ends of the V go off the edge of the apple skin. Slide your knife just under the skin of the opposite end of the apple and peel the apple up to the apex of the V. Remove the cut peel, and you're left with a little apple bunny with red ears and head! Repeat this process with each apple wedge, coating them on all sides with the salt water as you go to preserve them for a few hours.

THIS FOOD ALSO APPEARS IN . . .

- *Vampire Princess Miyu*
- *Sengoku Paradise Kiwami*
- *YuruYuri: Happy Go Lily*
- *Sailor Moon*
- *Cardcaptor Sakura*
- *Vividred Operation*
- *A-Channel*
- *The Qwaser of Stigmata*
- *Neighborhood Story*
- *Miss Kobayashi's Dragon Maid*
- *NAMUAMIDA-BUTSU! -UTENA-*

TAKO SAUSAGES

Another cute bento side often seen in anime is tako-san, which means "mister octopus," *tako* being the Japanese word for "octopus." These are small sausages cut to resemble a comical octopus and are a cute way to add protein to your bento.

1 sausage, wiener, or hot dog, cut into 3-inch segments, or use mini Vienna sausages

1 teaspoon vegetable or canola oil

Black or white sesame seeds, for eyes (optional)

Cheese slice, for mouth (optional)

Kewpie mayonnaise, for mouth (optional)

1 Starting 1 inch down from the rounded end of the sausage, cut the sausage in half lengthwise. Rotate the sausage and cut again 1 inch down lengthwise, creating 4 "legs." Cut these legs each in half, creating 8 legs. Using kitchen scissors instead of a knife also works well.

2 Spread the oil around a medium pan over medium heat and lay the cut sausages in the pan. Cook, stirring around to heat evenly, until the legs curl up. Transfer to a paper towel to absorb excess oil. Alternatively, you can boil the sausages if they are precooked. Simply place the cut sausage in a small pot of boiling water and cook until the legs curl up. Dry on a paper towel. You can also microwave precooked sausages in water for 1 to 1½ minutes.

3 If you'd like to put little faces on your tako sausages, use a toothpick to poke two shallow holes for eyes, then use the toothpick to press two sesame seeds into the premade holes so the seeds still show. To make a mouth, use a wide straw (like a smoothie straw) to cut a circle from a thin slice of cheese, then use a smaller, regular straw to cut a hole from the center of that circle to create a ring. Use a toothpick to smear on just a tiny bit of mayonnaise to "glue" the cheese ring onto the tako sausage for a mouth.

THIS FOOD ALSO APPEARS IN . . .

- *Sailor Moon*
- *Tonari no Seki-kun: The Master of Killing Time*
- *Tamagotchi!*
- *ReLIFE*
- *Karin*
- *Monthly Girls' Nozaki-Kun*
- *Junjo Romantica*
- *My Little Monster*
- *Blue Exorcist*
- *Kaguya-sama: Love Is War*
- *A Lull in the Sea*

OHITASHI

SERVES 6

1 (12-ounce) bunch spinach
⅓ cup Dashi Stock (page 56)
1 tablespoon soy sauce
2 teaspoons mirin
Katsuobushi (bonito) flakes, for garnish (optional)
White sesame seeds, for garnish (optional)

1 Bring enough water to cover the spinach to a boil in a large pot over high heat. Fill a large bowl halfway with water and add several ice cubes to create an ice bath. Add the spinach to the boiling water, stems first, then curling the leaves down into the pot, and cook for 30 seconds, or until bright green and limp. Drain the spinach and immediately place in the ice bath to cool. Drain again, gather the spinach so the leaves face in the same direction, squeeze gently, then pat with paper towels. Cut ½ inch of the stems off, then cut the spinach leaves into 2-inch lengths, placing each little bundle in a small serving bowl.

2 In a small bowl, stir together the dashi, soy sauce, and mirin. Pour the mixture evenly over each spinach serving. Top each serving with katsuobushi flakes or a sprinkling of sesame seeds, if desired. Great as a side dish to a meal or in a bento.

NOTE This version of ohitashi is called ohitashi horenso, horenso being the Japanese word for "spinach." You can substitute a variety of other greens, such as green beans, kale, okra, asparagus, Napa cabbage, bok choy, broccoli or broccolini, and more.

GOMA-AE

In animation and illustration, ohitashi can strongly resemble another common Japanese side dish called goma-ae. Goma-ae means "sesame" and "sauce," respectively, and is a dish made with a roasted sesame-seed dressing mixed with the same greens as ohitashi. It can be very hard to tell these two apart in 2D!

Blanch the spinach and place it in an ice bath as in the recipe above. Toast ¼ cup sesame seeds over medium heat until fragrant. Grind the seeds to a cornmeal-like consistency. Stir in 2 teaspoons each sugar, mirin, and soy sauce until a paste is formed. Spoon this mixture over the spinach and toss to coat. You can make this same sesame dressing to put on other types of blanched greens.

THIS FOOD ALSO APPEARS IN . . .

- *Yuri!!! on Ice*
- *K-On! The Movie*
- *The Great Passage*
- *Kuma Miko: Girl Meets Bear*
- *Myriad Colors Phantom World*
- *Witchy PreCure!*
- *Hanasaku Iroha: Blossoms for Tomorrow*
- *Kuromukuro*
- *Sakura Quest*
- *Erased*
- *Sweetness & Lightning*

KYURI ASAZUKE

SERVES 4

½ English cucumber, skin left on

½ teaspoon salt

1 (2 x 1-inch) piece dried kombu kelp

1 Cut the end off the cucumber half, then cut the cucumber diagonally into ¼-inch-wide oval slices. Place the slices in a medium bowl and toss with the salt. Using kitchen scissors, cut the kombu into very thin strips and toss with the salted cucumber slices.

2 Place a sheet of plastic wrap directly onto the cucumber slices and place a small plate on top. Set a canned good on the plate to weigh down the cucumber slices, then place the bowl in the refrigerator for 1 to 3 hours, depending on how flavorful you like your pickles (the longer, the more flavor). To serve, remove the weight and plastic and drain the pickles. Use as a side dish for a meal or in bento.

NOTE This recipe is very simple but also customizable. If you'd like some kick, add half of a small dried red chili pepper, chopped and seeds removed, when you add the kombu. You could also add a pinch of mustard powder, ginger powder or finely grated fresh ginger, or rice vinegar. Katsuobushi (bonito) flakes make for an umami addition.

FOOD FACTS *Kyuri* is the Japanese word for "cucumber" and *asazuke* means "to pickle shallowly" or "lightly," meaning to pickle something for a short time. Kyuri asazuke is a type of tsukemono or "pickled thing." Tsukemono are a very common side dish in Japanese meals, and come in many varieties using different ingredients and pickling methods. Daikon pickles are a common tsukemono (see page 72). Other ingredients are Napa cabbage (as seen in *Yuri!!! on Ice*), eggplant, carrots, lotus root, ginger (like beni shoga and sushi ginger), and Japanese plums (for umeboshi).

Japanese cucumbers are similar to English or hothouse cucumbers and Persian cucumbers. They don't have large seeds and the skin isn't bitter, so there's no need to peel them.

In summertime in Japan you can find whole cucumber kyuri asazuke on a stick sold by street vendors and at festivals to refresh you in the heat.

CUCUMBERS WITH MISO PASTE

In *Barakamon* we see another type of cucumber pickle; this miso paste pickling style is called misozuke.

In a shallow bowl, cut a cucumber into ⅛-inch-wide slices and toss with ½ teaspoon of salt. Place a sheet of plastic and a weighted plate on top, and let sit for at least 20 minutes to get out excess moisture. Uncover, drain, rinse, and pat with paper towels. Stir together 1 tablespoon of shiro (white) miso paste (or more if you'd like) and ½ teaspoon of sugar in a medium bowl. Add the cucumbers, massaging everything together with your hands. Serve immediately or cover and let sit for at least 30 minutes for the flavors to meld more. This can be a side dish or you can put it on top of a bowl of rice, donburi-style, like in *Barakamon*.

CULTURE FACTS Did you know that cucumbers are the favorite food of the mythical Japanese water demons called kappa? There is a cucumber sushi roll called kappamaki, or "kappa roll," because of this. *Kappa* means "river child" in Japanese, and, originally feared as violent beings, in modern times these creatures are often depicted as benign or humorous, like in *Sarazanmai* (watch your butt!), *Yokai Watch*, *Summer Days with Coo*, *GeGeGe no Kitaro*, *Nagasarete Airanto*, and many other anime. You can find kappamaki in *Sarazanmai*, *How to Keep a Mummy*, and *Galaxy Angel*.

KAPPAMAKI

A kappamaki is a hosomaki, or "thin roll."

Lay ½ sheet of sushi nori seaweed (4 x 7½-inches) lengthwise on a sushi mat. Wet your hands and spread ⅓ cup of sushi rice (see page 52) in an even layer over the seaweed, leaving 1 inch clear at the end farthest from you. Place a ½ x 7½-inch seedless cucumber stick (or smaller sticks equaling that size) in the center of the rice. Starting from the end closest to you and using the sushi mat to help, roll the seaweed and rice over to the opposite end, covering the cucumber as you go. Use the sushi mat to tighten and compact the roll. Slice the roll with a sharp wet knife into 6 to 8 equal pieces.

THIS FOOD ALSO APPEARS IN . . .

- *Mix: Meisei Story*
- *O Maidens in Your Savage Season*
- *The Devil is a Part-Timer!*
- *Clean Freak! Aoyama-kun*
- *Future Diary*
- *Restaurant to Another World*
- *The Great Passage*
- *Poco's Udon World*
- *Joshiraku*
- *The Qwaser of Stigmata*
- *Gourmet Girl Graffiti*
- *Isekai Izakaya: Japanese Food from Another World*

YAKISOBA

Stir-Fried Noodles

SERVES 1 TO 2 Sent to live in the country with her strict grandmother, city girl Ohana Matsumae begins to work at her grandmother's old-fashioned hot-spring inn, butting heads with the other employees and confronting her shortcomings. As time passes and she gets to know the staff better, Ohana eventually softens and comes to terms with her situation and self, deciding to work hard to become a better person. One evening, surrounded by lantern lights under the starry sky, amid people "festing it up," Ohana and Koichi Tanemura, her best friend and the boy who loves her, are served a special dish of yakisoba.

2 tablespoons Worcestershire sauce
1 tablespoon oyster sauce
2 teaspoons ketchup
1 teaspoon sugar
½ teaspoon soy sauce
2 large green cabbage leaves
½ large carrot
¼ medium onion
3 strips bacon
3 ounces dried noodles, such as ramen
2 teaspoons plus 1 tablespoon vegetable or canola oil
Aonori powdered seaweed, for garnish (optional)
Beni shoga pickled ginger, squeezed of excess liquid, for garnish (optional)
Katsuobushi (bonito) flakes, for garnish (optional)

1 Whisk together the Worcestershire sauce, oyster sauce, ketchup, sugar, and soy sauce in a small bowl until completely combined. Set aside until needed.

2 Slice away the hard parts of the cabbage leaves, then lay the leaves on top of one another and chop into 1-inch pieces. Peel the carrot and cut it in half widthwise. Cut each half lengthwise into thin rectangle slices. Stack a few slices at a time and cut them into ¼-inch-wide strips. Julienne the onion into thin strips. Stack the bacon strips and cut them into 1-inch-wide pieces.

3 In a medium pan over high heat, bring 2 cups water to a boil and add the dry noodles. Cook, stirring occasionally, for 3 minutes, or until cooked through. Remove the pot from the heat. Strain the noodles and toss them in the strainer to get rid of excess moisture. Place the noodles back in the pot and coat with 2 teaspoons of oil to keep them from sticking together.

4 Heat 1 tablespoon of oil in a large pan or skillet over medium-high heat. Add the bacon and cook until it's no longer pink. Add the cabbage, carrot, and onion and toss together to coat with oil. Using two spatulas is the most common way to cook yakisoba. Add the prepared noodles once the cabbage leaves are just beginning to wilt and toss all of the ingredients together to distribute them among the noodles. If the noodles are clumping together, add ½ teaspoon more oil.

5 Pour the prepared sauce over the mixture and toss everything again to coat evenly. Spread the yakisoba across the pan to heat it evenly and cook until the sauce is beginning to caramelize and stick to the pan. Scrape up the caramelized sauce and mix it in with the noodles. Turn off the heat and transfer the yakisoba to a serving dish. As optional garnishes, sprinkle the yakisoba with aonori seaweed and top with beni shoga and katsuobushi flakes.

FOOD FACTS *Yaki* means "grilled," and *soba* means "noodles." Historically all noodles were called soba; for example, ramen noodles were called *chuka soba*, meaning "Chinese noodles" (which are recommended here).

Yakisoba pan is a variant of yakisoba that you can see in *K-On!*, *Goldfish Warning!*, *Given*, *Boruto: Naruto Next Generations*, *Rin-ne*, *Gintama*, *Yamada-kun and the Seven Witches*, *Hiiro no Kakera: The Tamayori Princess Saga*, and many more anime. *Pan* is the Japanese word for bread, borrowed from Portuguese, and yakisoba pan is yakisoba noodles stuffed into a split-top roll. It's very popular among students as a hearty and easy-to-grab meal, especially at lunchtime.

To make your own yakisoba pan, use half the amount of noodles but the same amount of sauce. You can omit the vegetables and bacon or use half amounts of those as well. Butter the cut inside of a split-top roll and pack the noodles in. You can include the garnish or not. Sometimes yakisoba pan is even topped with half a hard-boiled egg. Wrap the yakisoba pan tightly in plastic wrap until ready to eat.

There's a variation of yakisoba pan called omusoba pan, seen in *The World God Only Knows*, that includes a thin egg omelet wrapped around the middle of the yakisoba pan like a belly warmer.

CULTURE FACTS The Yunosagi Onsen in *Hanasaku Iroha* is closely based on the real-world Yuwaku Onsen in the town of Kanazawa in Ishikawa Prefecture. After destructive flooding and landslides in 2009, the animation studio P.A.Works collaborated with Kanazawa officials to come up with a way to boost the town's economy and citizenship—thus *Hanasaku Iroha* was born in 2011. The setting for this special yakisoba is the local Bonburi Festival, which celebrates the story of a goddess being guided by bonburi lanterns to the yearly gathering of the gods. Townspeople write their wishes on little wooden plaques that are later burned to send those wishes to the heavens, and those who hold their lanterns up for the procession will have their wishes granted by the grateful goddess. This beautiful festival may have been created for the anime, but to celebrate the final episode of the series, the town of Kanazawa actually held the festival in real life—sparking the creation of the annual Bonburi Festival that has been held there ever since, bringing in people from all over Japan and the world.

THIS FOOD ALSO APPEARS IN . . .

- *Trickster*
- *Starmyu*
- *Amanchu!*
- *Aikatsu Stars!*
- *Silver Spoon*
- *Love Live! Sunshine!!*
- *Full Metal Panic!*
- *Log Horizon*
- *K-On!*
- *Ninjaboy Rantaro*
- *The World God Only Knows*
- *Digimon Adventure tri. 2: Determination*

WOLF CHILDREN

YAKITORI

Grilled Skewered Chicken

MAKES 8 SKEWERS While attending her college lectures, Hana meets a mysterious young man and they quickly fall in love, despite the fact that the man can change into a wolf. They create a simple life together, sharing modest meals like yakitori cooked over a small indoor grill at home, and eventually welcome the birth of two rambunctious half-wolf pups.

- **8 wooden skewers**
- **¼ cup soy sauce**
- **¼ cup mirin**
- **¼ cup sake**
- **2 tablespoons dark brown sugar**
- **2 tablespoons cold water**
- **1 teaspoon cornstarch**
- **Vegetable or canola oil, for grilling**
- **1½ pounds boneless chicken thighs or breast**
- **Salt and freshly ground black pepper**
- **1 green bell pepper, stem and core removed, chopped into 1-inch pieces**
- **1 red bell pepper, stem and core removed, chopped into 1-inch pieces**
- **1 yellow bell pepper, stem and core removed, chopped into 1-inch pieces**
- **1 medium sweet onion, peeled and chopped into 1-inch pieces**

1 Soak wooden skewers in water for at least 30 minutes before grilling.

2 In a small pot over medium heat, whisk together the soy sauce, mirin, sake, and brown sugar. In a small bowl, whisk together the water and cornstarch until well combined, then whisk this mixture into the soy sauce mixture. Bring the mixture to a boil, then reduce the heat to medium-low and simmer for 8 to 10 minutes, stirring often, until thickened. Remove from the heat and let cool for 5 minutes before pouring into a narrow glass for dipping.

3 Heat a grill to medium-high and brush the grate with oil, or heat a large pan on the stovetop on medium-high and brush with oil.

4 Rinse the chicken in cold water and pat dry with paper towels. Cut the chicken into 1½-inch pieces, season it with salt and pepper, and toss to coat.

5 Thread the chicken, peppers, and onion on the soaked skewers in alternating patterns, leaving at least 2 inches of free space at the bottom of the skewers for handling.

6 Lay the prepared skewers side-by-side on the grill or pan and cook for 5 minutes. Use tongs to turn the skewers to the opposite side and cook for another 5 minutes. If you'd like to brush on some of the prepared sauce, do so now and cook an additional minute per side.

7 Transfer the cooked skewers to a serving plate and serve with the glass of sauce on the side for dipping.

FOOD FACTS Yakitori can be served with or without sauce. Often the salty-sweet sauce, or "tare," is brushed on while the chicken is grilling, or the chicken is simply seasoned with salt and the sauce is used for dipping once served, or no sauce is used at all. Tare sauce is like teriyaki (*tare* plus *yaki*) and is meant to add flavor and shine to the meat.

Yakitori is a type of kushiyaki, which breaks down to "skewer" and "grill," and refers to any skewered and grilled food. There are various types of kushiyaki using different kinds of meat, vegetables, tofu, and more, but yakitori specifically refers to grilled chicken (though sometimes yakitori is said in a broad sense, interchangeable with the word *kushiyaki*). There are different kinds of yakitori using various types of chicken meat, such as breast ("mune") and breast tenderloin ("sasami"; *Tenchi Muyo!*, anyone?), thigh ("momo"), ground chicken ("tsukune") as in *Bunny Drop* and *Case Closed*, chicken skin ("kawa"), and more. Another popular type of yakitori seen often in anime is "negima" or "torinegi," which is chicken and leek, or Japanese green onion. You can find this in *Anonymous Noise*, *Classroom of the Elite*, *Love Live! Sunshine!!*, *Himouto! Umaru-chan*, *Utawarerumono: The False Faces*, and many more. Negima and chicken on its own are the most common forms of yakitori.

CULTURE FACTS Yakitori is a very popular street food, and there are even whole restaurants dedicated to it. If you're in a group, make sure you don't double dip—that's very bad manners in Japan!

THIS FOOD ALSO APPEARS IN . . .

- *Space Dandy*
- *Wakakozake*
- *Bungo Stray Dogs*
- *Polar Bear Café*
- *Beck: Mongolian Chop Squad*
- *TsukiPro the Animation*
- *When Supernatural Battles Became Commonplace*
- *Psycho-Pass: Sinners of the System Case.2*
- *Blast of Tempest*
- *Laid-Back Camp*
- *Hakata Mentai! Pirikarako-chan*
- *Wotakoi: Love Is Hard for Otaku*
- *Interviews with Monster Girls*
- *Is It Wrong to Try to Pick Up Girls in a Dungeon?*
- *Sakura Quest*
- *Utawarerumono: The False Faces*
- *Love Live! Sunshine!!*
- *Classroom of the Elite*
- *Anonymous Noise*

MOB PSYCHO 100

TAKOYAKI

Pancake Balls with Octopus

SERVES 2 Powerfully psychic, emotionally dormant, and socially innocent adolescent Shigeo Kageyama, nicknamed Mob, begins working for fake psychic and con man (and excellent massage therapist) Reigen Arataka under the pretense of master and apprentice, unaware that Reigan doesn't have a psychic bone in his body. Throughout the course of their partnership—which truly is one of master and student at times—Reigan fakes his way through numerous spiritual encounters (with Mob saving his bacon countless times) and the occasional too-hot takoyaki.

- **2 tablespoons Mentsuyu (page 26)**
- **1½ tablespoons Worcestershire sauce**
- **1 tablespoon ketchup**
- **2 teaspoons sugar**
- **1 tablespoon minced beni shoga pickled ginger**
- **1 large egg, at room temperature**
- **¾ cup Dashi Stock (page 56)**
- **½ cup cake flour**
- **Vegetable or canola oil, for frying**
- **½ cup chopped boiled octopus**
- **2 tablespoons tenkasu tempura bits (see page 15)**
- **2 tablespoons minced green onion**
- **Kewpie mayonnaise, for garnish**
- **Aonori powdered seaweed, for garnish**
- **Katsuobushi (bonito) flakes, for garnish**

1 In a small bowl, whisk together the mentsuyu, Worcestershire sauce, ketchup, and sugar. Set aside until needed. Squeeze the beni shoga in a paper towel to get rid of excess moisture and set aside.

2 Whisk together the egg and dashi in a medium bowl, then sift in the cake flour and whisk until smooth. Pour this batter into a liquid measuring cup with a pour spout.

3 Heat a takoyaki pan over medium heat and oil it generously. You can also use an electric cake pop maker if you don't have a takoyaki pan.

4 Pour the batter into the round portions of the pan, filling them up; it's okay if the batter overflows. Drop 1 to 2 pieces of octopus into each cup along with sprinkles of the reserved beni shoga, the tenkasu, and green onion. Cook for 3 minutes.

5 Using 2 wooden skewers or takoyaki picks, turn each half dome 90 degrees, gathering in the extra batter around it and stuffing it into the cup. Pour a little bit of batter into each cup to fill it again and rotate so that the rounded bottom of the cooked batter is on top. Cook for another 3 minutes.

6 Rotate the balls to make sure they're round and cooked all over—golden brown and crispy on the outside. Turn off the heat and transfer the takoyaki to 2 serving dishes, 6 to a dish.

7 Brush the prepared sauce over the takoyaki and top with a zigzag of Kewpie mayonnaise and sprinklings of aonori and katsuobushi. Eat with small wooden picks or toothpicks.

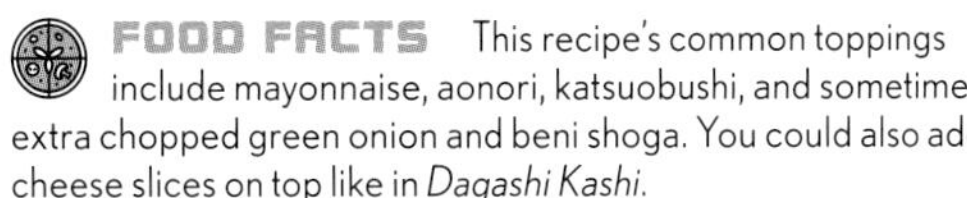

FOOD FACTS This recipe's common toppings include mayonnaise, aonori, katsuobushi, and sometimes extra chopped green onion and beni shoga. You could also add cheese slices on top like in *Dagashi Kashi*.

ANIME FACT Shigeo's nickname "Mob" comes from *mobu*, which means "minor character" in Japanese, denoting his unassuming look and manners, and hiding the twist that he is anything but!

THIS FOOD ALSO APPEARS IN . . .

- *One Piece*
- *Tsuredure Children*
- *Tsukigakurei*
- *Kabukibu!*
- *Hinako Note*
- *No Game No Life*
- *Gabriel Dropout*
- *Modest Heroes*
- *One-Punch Man*
- *Diabolik Lovers*
- *Shirobako*
- *Wolf Girl & Black Prince*
- *Cardcaptor Sakura*
- *Pretty Cure All Stars DX*
- *Waiting in the Summer*
- *RobiHachi*
- *Dino Girl Gauko*
- *Hundred*
- *YuruYuri: Happy Go Lily*
- *Nyaruko: Crawling with Love!*
- *Penguindrum*
- *Soul Eater NOT!*
- *Log Horizon*

RANMA ½

OKONOMIYAKI

Savory Cabbage Pancake

SERVES 1 TO 2 Cursed (and blessed) to turn into a girl every time he's doused with cold water, teenage martial artist Ranma Saotome has acquired a bevy of fiancées over the years, thanks both to misunderstandings and to his father, Genma (who turns into a panda), promising him in marriage for his own benefit. One such fiancée, Ukyo Kuonji, who was Ranma's childhood friend and was betrothed in exchange for her father's okonomiyaki cart, tracks Ranma and Genma down and fights them using okonomiyaki-inspired martial arts—and even okonomiyaki itself!

1 tablespoon ketchup
2 teaspoons Worcestershire sauce
1½ teaspoons oyster sauce
1½ teaspoons sugar
2 tablespoons chopped beni shoga pickled ginger, plus more for garnish
2 cups finely shredded green cabbage
¼ cup Dashi Stock (page 56) or water
1 large egg
½ cup cake flour
Pinch of baking powder
2 tablespoons grated yamaimo, nagaimo, or golden yam (optional)
1 tablespoon vegetable or canola oil
½ cup chopped green onions, plus more for garnish
⅓ cup tenkasu tempura bits (see page 15)
3 slices bacon
Kewpie mayonnaise, for garnish
Aonori powdered seaweed, for garnish
Katsuobushi (bonito) flakes, for garnish

1 In a small bowl, whisk together the ketchup, Worcestershire sauce, oyster sauce, and sugar. Set aside until needed.

2 Squeeze the beni shoga in a paper towel and lay the shredded cabbage in a single layer between a few paper towels, to get rid of excess moisture. Set aside.

3 In a medium bowl, whisk together the dashi stock and egg. Sift in the flour and baking powder and whisk until the batter is smooth. If you're using the grated yam, whisk it in until combined.

4 Heat the oil in a skillet or large pan over medium heat. Stir the reserved beni shoga, the green onions, and tenkasu into the batter until evenly distributed, then fold in the reserved cabbage.

5 Scoop the batter into the hot pan and spread it out into a circle ½ inch thick, using a spatula to round out and shape the edges. Lay the bacon strips on top, closely together, folding them as needed, and then cover the pan with a lid and cook for 3 minutes. Use 2 spatulas to carefully flip the okonomiyaki over, cover, and cook for another 5 minutes. Flip again and leave the pan uncovered this time, letting the okonomiyaki cook for an additional 2 minutes.

6 Use the 2 spatulas to transfer the okonomiyaki to a serving plate, then brush the top with the reserved sauce. Squeeze mayonnaise over the okonomiyaki in a zigzag or spiral pattern, and add sprinkles of aonori, katsuobushi, and extra beni shoga and green onions, if desired. Serve for 1 person, or cut in half for 2.

NOTE If you don't have a squeeze bottle of mayonnaise, you can scoop some mayo into a plastic sandwich bag and snip a little hole in one corner. If you'd like to make a pattern on the okonomiyaki, drag a toothpick or skewer shallowly through the mayo pattern.

FOOD FACTS In the *Ranma ½* manga, the chapter that introduces Ukyo is titled "'Okonomiyaki' means 'I love you.'" Actually, it means "grilled as you like it"! There are two main versions of okonomiyaki: Osaka-style, in which the ingredients are mixed together before cooking (this recipe), and Hiroshima-style, which includes noodles, and the ingredients are added in layers while cooking.

THIS FOOD ALSO APPEARS IN . . .

- *Yowamushi Pedal*
- *True Tears*
- *Grand Blue Dreaming*
- *Cardcaptor Sakura: Clear Card*
- *Atom: the Beginning*
- *Sweetness & Lightning*
- *Kuroko's Basketball*
- *Kimi ni Todoke: From Me to You*
- *Non Non Biyori Repeat*
- *Dagashi Kashi*
- *Celestial Method*
- *Charlotte*
- *Shirobako*
- *The Rolling Girls*
- *Saki*

KILL LA KILL

KOROKKE

Breaded and Deep-Fried Potato Cakes

SERVES 4 While looking for her father's killer, Scissor Blade–toting high schooler Ryuko Matoi transfers to Honnouji Academy, where certain students don superpowered Goku Uniforms. Obtaining a special uniform of her own, Ryuko battles the student council, finds answers to the mystery surrounding her life, and is befriended by loyal ditz Mako Mankanshoku, whose family takes Ryuko in and shares their special mystery korokke with her.

- **1 large Russet potato, peeled and diced into ½-inch cubes**
- **½ tablespoon butter**
- **¼ teaspoon salt**
- **⅛ teaspoon pepper**
- **1 tablespoon vegetable or canola oil, plus more for deep-frying**
- **¼ medium onion, minced**
- **⅓ pound lean ground beef or pork, or a mixture of both**
- **1 teaspoon sugar**
- **2 teaspoons soy sauce**
- **¼ cup all-purpose flour**
- **1 large egg, beaten well**
- **1 cup panko**
- **Tonkatsu Sauce (page 35), for serving (optional)**

1 Cover the potato pieces in water in a large pot and bring to a boil over high heat. Cook until the pieces are easily pierced with a fork, 10 to 15 minutes. Drain the potato pieces well and return them to the pot over medium heat, shaking the pot to evaporate excess water.

2 Transfer the potatoes to a large bowl and add the butter, salt, and pepper. Mash together until the mixture becomes cohesive, like dough.

3 Heat the oil in a large pan over medium heat. Add the onion and cook until just tender, about 3 minutes. Add the meat, sugar, and soy sauce and cook until the meat is no longer pink, about 5 minutes, breaking it up into small bits as it cooks. Drain the meat if needed, then lay it on a baking sheet lined with several paper towels. Cover the top of the meat with paper towels as well and pat to get rid of excess grease.

4 Stir the meat into the mashed potatoes until evenly distributed. Shape the mixture into an even round and cut it into 6 equal segments. Shape each segment into a flattened oval, about 1 inch thick. Lay these on a baking sheet and chill in the refrigerator for 15 minutes to solidify.

5 Heat 1 inch of oil to 350°F in a large pan. Set out 3 shallow bowls. Put the flour in one, the egg in another, and the panko in the third. Remove the potato cakes from the refrigerator and begin coating them, first in flour, then in egg, then in panko. Pat the potato cakes to make sure the panko stays on well, then place them on the baking sheet.

6 Once the oil reaches the right temperature, lower 2 to 3 korokke into the hot oil, making sure not to overcrowd the pan. Cook until the bottom is golden and crispy, then turn over and cook the other side. Transfer the finished korokke to a wire cooling rack set over a baking sheet lined with paper towels. Remove any bits of panko from the oil as you go. Repeat with all of the korokke. Serve warm, with tonkatsu sauce, if desired.

NOTE To save money, the Mankanshoku family fills their korokke with pretty much anything they can get their hands on. If you'd like to add other ingredients to your korokke, go right ahead—you can make it like a korokke roulette! Some ideas for fillings are chopped cooked shrimp, diced mushrooms, buttered corn kernels, minced carrot with peas, diced ham and shredded cheese, furikake rice seasoning, diced cooked chicken and broccoli, chopped pickled herring . . . you can really have a lot of fun with it. If you do use ground meat, as in the recipe above, you can flavor it differently with seasonings such as nutmeg, curry powder, or even taco seasoning.

FOOD FACTS Korokke is the Japanese version of the French croquette and is a common street food, festival food, and home-cooked meal. Another popular way to eat korokke is korokke pan, which is a sandwich using a split-top roll. You can see this in *Atom: the Beginning*, where the characters like to dip their korokke pan in udon soup (page 26). In *Your Name* we even see two korokke in a floppy egg salad sandwich.

Menchi katsu looks very similar to korokke, as it's breaded and crispy outside, but is made of a minced meat patty on the inside; *menchi* means "minced" and *katsu* is short for "cutlet." You can see this version in *Isekai Izakaya: Japanese Food from Another World* and *Restaurant to Another World.*

THIS FOOD ALSO APPEARS IN . . .

- *Is It Wrong to Try to Pick Up Girls in a Dungeon?*
- *Dino Girl Gauko*
- *My Love Story!!*
- *Stars Align*
- *Star Driver*
- *Amagi Brilliant Park*
- *Maken-Ki! Battling Venus*
- *Majikoi: Oh! Samurai Girls*
- *The Rolling Girls*
- *Tsugumomo*
- *Kuroko's Basketball*
- *World Trigger*
- *Beelzebub*
- *Flying Witch*
- *Listen to Me, Girls, I'm Your Father!*
- *C3–Cube x Cursed x Curious*

SILVER SPOON

YAKI TOMOROKOSHI

Grilled Corn with Soy Sauce

SERVES 4 Yuugo Hachiken pushed himself hard in school but never felt good enough when measured against his parents' expectations. To escape his perceived failure and suffocating home life, and with no real plan for his future, Hachiken enrolls in Ooezo Agricultural High School, a boarding school in the countryside of Hokkaido. He soon realizes that the practical aspects of the school's classes are more demanding than he imagined, but he makes friends with his classmates and gains confidence and a sense of purpose. During a break he even goes to work on a classmate's farm and further learns the value of hard work, responsibility, and freshly picked corn grilled with a splash of soy sauce.

3 tablespoons soy sauce
2 tablespoons mirin
1 tablespoon sugar
1 tablespoon butter
4 ears sweet corn
Vegetable or canola oil, for grilling
Shichimi togarashi Japanese pepper seasoning (optional)

1 In a small pot over medium heat, combine the soy sauce, mirin, and sugar and cook until the sugar is dissolved. Remove the pot from the heat and whisk in the butter. Set aside.

2 Shuck the corn by peeling off the husks and pulling off the silk strands under very warm running water.

3 Bring a large pot of water (enough to cover the corn) to a boil over high heat. If the corn is too long for your pot, cut the cobs in half. Place the corn in the pot and cook for 3 minutes. Drain and pat the corn dry with paper towels.

4 Heat a grill or large pan over medium-high heat and brush oil onto the grill grate or pan. Add the corn cobs and cook for 5 minutes on each side, using tongs to rotate.

5 Once the corn has many browned kernels all over, re-whisk the prepared sauce and brush it onto the corn. Roll the corn onto the brushed side and cook for 2 minutes. Brush on more sauce and rotate the corn again and cook for another 2 minutes, repeating for each side. Remove the corn from the heat and transfer to a serving dish. Sprinkle with the shichimi togarashi seasoning, if desired.

NOTE To skewer your yaki tomorokoshi like Japanese festival vendors sometimes do: If you're grilling your corn, after the cobs are removed from the boiling water, cut ½ inch from the bottom of each, using a pot holder to hold them steady, as they will be hot. Push a sturdy wooden chopstick up through the center of each cob, just until the stick is in firmly. If you're cooking the corn in a pan, cut ½ inch from the bottom of each cob after being boiled, then wait until *after* they're cooked and sauced in the pan before inserting the chopsticks.

FOOD FACTS Some people simply brush soy sauce over the grilled corn, and others add miso paste to the sauce, or make a concoction of miso paste, sugar, and butter.

ANIME FACTS The title *K-On!* or "kei-on" is short for *keiongaku*, which means "light" or "contemporary" music in Japanese, which is the type of music the girls in Ho-kago ("After School") Tea Time play in the show.

THIS FOOD ALSO APPEARS IN . . .

- *K-On!*
- *Charlotte*
- *Toriko*
- *Amanchu!*
- *March Comes in Like a Lion*
- *School Babysitters*
- *Arpeggio of Blue Steel*
- *Minky Momo: The Bridge Over Dreams*
- *Ninjaboy Rantaro*
- *Ranma ½*
- *Waiting in the Summer*
- *Natsume's Book of Friends*
- *THE IDOLM@STER*
- *Inari Kon Kon*
- *Gourmet Girl Graffiti*
- *Aikatsu Stars!*
- *Smile PreCure!*
- *Yumeiro Patissiere SP Professional*
- *C3–Cube x Cursed x Curious*
- *Atom: the Beginning*
- *Your Name*

DRAGON BALL

NIKUMAN

Steamed Pork-Filled Buns

MAKES 8 Raised on Earth and taught martial arts as a child, Saiyan Son Goku travels the planet to become a powerful fighter while looking for the titular Dragon Balls. He meets a colorful cast of characters who help and hinder him along the way, enters martial arts tournaments to get stronger, saves the planet numerous times, and gobbles up tons of food, such as towering bowls of rice, huge shanks of meat, bowls of ramen, and baskets of nikuman to keep up his strength!

2 cups all-purpose flour
2 tablespoons plus 2 teaspoons sugar
1 teaspoon instant dry yeast
¾ teaspoon salt
1 teaspoon baking powder
¾ cup warm water (110°F)
1 tablespoon vegetable or canola oil, plus more for greasing
1 cup minced green cabbage
¼ cup minced shiitake mushrooms
¼ cup minced green onion
2 tablespoons minced carrot
½ cup ground pork
½ cup minced pork belly
1 tablespoon soy sauce
1 tablespoon oyster sauce
1 tablespoon sesame oil
1 tablespoon sake
1 tablespoon cornstarch
1 teaspoon grated ginger
2 twists of freshly ground black pepper
Dipping sauce (see below; optional)

1 In the bowl of a stand mixer, whisk together the flour, 2 tablespoons of sugar, the instant yeast, ¼ teaspoon of salt, and baking powder. Make a well in the center and pour in the water and vegetable oil and mix with a dough hook attachment until you have a smooth and stretchy dough, about 10 minutes.

2 Lift the dough out of the bowl and shape into a ball. Lightly spread vegetable oil around the bowl and place the dough back in. Cover the bowl with plastic wrap and place in a warm place for 1 hour, or until the dough has doubled in size.

3 Meanwhile, prepare the filling. In a medium bowl, toss the cabbage with the remaining ½ teaspoon salt and let sit for 10 minutes. Drain and squeeze the cabbage to get rid of the excess moisture and pat dry with paper towels. Pat the mushrooms, green onion, and carrots with paper towels as well to avoid any extra moisture in the filling.

4 In a large bowl, combine the ground pork, pork belly, cabbage, mushrooms, green onions, carrot, soy sauce, oyster sauce, sesame oil, sake, cornstarch, ginger, and pepper. Use your hands to mix everything together thoroughly until the mixture is a pale paste. Cover with plastic wrap and chill in the refrigerator until needed.

5 Once the dough has risen, punch it down to deflate the air. Lightly dust a work surface with flour. Divide the dough into 8 equal wedges. Form each wedge into a ball and cover the balls with a large sheet of plastic wrap. Let rest for 10 minutes.

6 Meanwhile, cut eight 5-by-5-inch squares of parchment paper.

7 Remove the bowl of filling from the refrigerator. Working with 1 ball of dough at a time, roll it 4 inches across, making the edges thinner than the center. Scoop 2 tablespoons of filling into the center of the dough disk. Lift, pleat, and pinch the edges of the dough together, drawing the dough closed over the filling as you go. Twist the gathered dough at the top to close and seal. Place the bun on a square of parchment paper. Repeat this process with the rest of the dough and filling, covering the completed buns with plastic wrap. Once you're finished, let the buns rest for 20 minutes.

8 Pour 2 inches of water into a large pot over medium heat. If you have a steamer tray, place it in the pot, or if you have a bamboo steamer, place it over the pot. Wrap a kitchen towel around the pot or bamboo steamer lid, tying the ends at the top to keep them away from the heating element. If you don't have a steamer tray or bamboo steamer, make 3 golf ball–size balls of aluminum foil, place them in opposite sides of the pot, and balance a plate on top of the balls.

9 Once the pot is steaming, add 3 to 4 nikuman, keeping them 2 inches apart; you don't want to crowd them or they'll stick together. Steam for 15 minutes, then remove from the pot using tongs. Repeat with the rest of the nikuman. Serve warm as is or with a dipping sauce.

10 To store the nikuman, place them in an airtight container in the refrigerator for up to 2 days. To reheat a bun, wrap it in a damp paper towel, then wrap it loosely in plastic wrap, and microwave for 30 seconds. You can also freeze the nikuman by wrapping each bun in plastic wrap and placing them in a large freezer bag. To reheat a frozen bun, follow the same steps with the damp paper towel and plastic wrap, but microwave for 1 minute, then check and heat for another 15 to 30 seconds if needed.

NOTE For a quick dipping sauce, stir together 2 tablespoons soy sauce and 1 tablespoon rice vinegar. Add in a couple drops of la-yu oil if you'd like it spicy.

FOOD FACTS Nikuman is a combination of the word *niku* for "meat" and *man* from another steamed, filled dough bun called manju. Manju came from the Chinese "mantou" steamed bun, which can be filled or not. Over time, to differentiate between filled and non-filled mantou, the name "boazi" was given to the former, which is what nikuman is based on. Because of this connection, nikuman is sometimes called "chukaman," with "chuka" referring to something that is Chinese. Like many other fusion foods, the flavor has been adapted to Japanese tastes.

Is this what Lin and Sen are eating in *Spirited Away* while overlooking the nighttime ocean at the bathhouse? Or is it anman, which uses the same dough as nikuman but is filled with Anko Sweet Red Bean Paste (page 99) instead? Both are yummy, but the nikuman would be better for a meal. Did you know there is also a bun in this style called pizzaman filled with—you guessed it—pizza toppings?

ANIME FACTS *Dragon Ball* is greatly inspired by the epic Chinese tale of the Monkey King called *Journey to the West*. Remember little Goku's tail? And his full-on mega-monkey mode?

THIS FOOD ALSO APPEARS IN . . .

- *THE IDOLM@STER*
- *Kanon*
- *Rin-ne*
- *Cardcaptor Sakura*
- *Ranma ½*
- *The Story of Saiunkoku*
- *A Town Where You Live*
- *Planet With*
- *Inuyasha*
- *Hime-chan's Ribbon*
- *Hayate the Combat Butler*
- *Neon Genesis Evangelion*
- *Gintama*
- *You and Me*
- *Nichijou—My Ordinary Life*
- *Bomberman Jetters*
- *Mysterious Girlfriend X*
- *Yuyushiki*

ASCENDANCE OF A BOOKWORM

JAGA BATA

Steamed Potato with Butter

SERVES 1 Avid book lover—and unfortunately recently deceased—Urano Motosu awakens in a different world . . . in the body of a five-year-old named Myne. She soon discovers that books in this world are very difficult to come by and vows to create books of her own. Despite her new body's frailty, and with the help of her new family and friends, she embarks on the task, braving numerous setbacks and enjoying successes as well. During the long process of papermaking, when the cold weather sets in, Myne introduces steamed potatoes and butter to her best friend and partner Lutz, to warm their freezing fingers.

1 medium potato, washed well, skin on
1 tablespoon butter
Salt

1 Cut an X into the potato, going only halfway through. Pour 1 inch of water into a medium pot, cover, and bring to a boil over medium heat. Place a steamer tray in the pot, or a bamboo steamer over the pot, then place the potato in, cut side up. Cover securely and steam for 30 minutes, adding more water as needed, until a skewer poked into a thick part of the potato goes in easily.

2 Remove the pot from the heat and use tongs to move the hot potato to a serving plate. Use a fork to open the potato on the X cuts and fluff it up inside, then place a pat of butter in the center. Season with salt.

NOTE If you don't have a steamer tray or bamboo steamer, you can scrunch up three golf ball–size balls of aluminum foil and float them in the pot with 1 inch of water. Place a small heatproof plate on top, making sure the plate bottom is not touching the water. Place the potato on the plate, put the lid on the pot, and continue with the recipe. You can also simply X-cut the potato, place it in a microwavable bowl, and cover in plastic wrap. Microwave for 5 minutes, or until cooked all the way through.

FOOD FACTS Jaga bata is a portmanteau of *jaga* from *jagaimo* meaning "potato" and *bata* for "butter." It's a simple but satisfying food often purchased from street vendors and at festivals, so warming and comforting in chilly weather.

Roasted Japanese sweet potatoes, simply called yaki imo, are also very popular when the cold weather hits, as seen in *Your Lie in April* and *Doraemon*. Sweet potatoes in Japan, known as satsumaimo, are very distinctive with their sweet taste, purple skin, and vibrant yellow centers when cooked.

ANIME FACTS *Ascendance of a Bookworm* is an example of the *isekai* genre, meaning "another world," where the main character somehow goes to a different world, usually retaining some or all of their knowledge. The earliest example of the isekai genre in Japan is the folktale of *Urashima Taro* (adapted into an anime film in 1918), in which a young man is transported to an undersea kingdom that runs on different time than the real world. In the case of *Ascendance of a Bookworm*, the transition is reincarnation into an already existing body. In *That Time I Got Reincarnated as a Slime*, it's straight-up reincarnation for the main character and summoning for others. In *The Twelve Kingdoms*, a character is whisked away by an otherworldly person—or, in the case of *Magic Knight Rayearth*, by flying fish; in *Fushigi Yuugi* it's through a book; in *Log Horizon* it's a video game becoming real; in *Endride* it's through a crystal; and in *Kyo Kara Maoh!* it's via a toilet! Isekai can also happen in reverse, with fantasy characters coming to the real world, like in *Re:Creators* and *Gate*.

THIS FOOD ALSO APPEARS IN . . .

- *Restaurant to Another World*
- *Aria the Origination*
- *Tantei Opera Milky Holmes*
- *Yumeiro Patissiere SP Professional*
- *Attack on Titan* (sans butter)

MY HERO ACADEMIA

TAIYAKI

Sweet Red Bean–Filled Fish-Shaped Cake

SERVES 8 In a world where almost everyone has a power, or "quirk," and being a hero is a profession, quirk-less young Izuku Midoriya nevertheless dreams of being a great hero like his superstring idol All Might. After an encounter with a villain in which All Might witnesses Midoriya's true hero spirit, Midoriya is on his way to fulfilling his dreams.

During training, Midoriya meets one of All Might's past teachers, the now elderly but still spritely and strong Gran Torino, whose favorite food is taiyaki. Midoriya learns quickly—you don't mess with Gran Torino's taiyaki!

1½ cups cake flour
½ teaspoon baking soda
½ teaspoon baking powder
Pinch of salt
1 large egg
2 tablespoons sugar
⅓ cup milk
2 tablespoons butter, melted
½ cup Anko Sweet Red Bean Paste (page 99)

1 Sift the flour, baking soda, baking powder, and salt into a medium bowl. In a separate bowl, whisk the egg and sugar until well incorporated, then whisk in the milk and ⅓ cup water. Make a well in the center of the flour mixture and slowly pour in the milk mixture, whisking until the batter is smooth. Cover the batter and let sit on the counter for 30 minutes.

2 If you're using an electric taiyaki maker, follow the appliance's instructions. If you're using a stovetop taiyaki pan, place the pan, open, over medium heat. Once the correct temperature has been reached, dip a folded paper towel into the melted butter and wipe both sides of the taiyaki pan. Leave the pan open.

3 Whisk the batter and add 2 tablespoons into one of the fish-shaped taiyaki molds, using a small spatula to quickly spread the mixture to coat the mold. Repeat with the second mold, leaving the pan open. Cook for 1 minute, then scoop 1 tablespoon of anko into each mold, spreading it out to the length of the mold.

4 Spoon another tablespoon of batter over the anko in both molds, adding more batter as needed (it's okay if the batter overflows a little). Close the pan and flip it over. Cook for 3 minutes, flip again, and cook for another minute. Remove from the heat once both sides of the taiyaki are golden brown.

THIS FOOD ALSO APPEARS IN . . .

- *Shugo Chara!! Doki*
- *Mikan Enkki*
- *Miss Kobayashi's Dragon Maid*
- *Princess Jellyfish*
- *Aikatsu Stars!*
- *Kanon*
- *Hinako Note*
- *THE IDOL-M@STER: Cinderella Girls*
- *Kannagi: Crazy Shrine Maidens*
- *To Love Ru*
- *My Little Monster*
- *Wake Up, Girls!*
- *Natsume's Book of Friends*
- *Sket Dance*
- *Shugo Chara!*
- *You and Me*
- *Orange*

LOG HORIZON

ANPAN

Bun with Sweet Red Bean Filling

MAKES 8 With the twelfth expansion to the MMORPG *Elder Tale*, thousands of players find themselves transported physically into the world of the game. Trapped graduate student Shiroe, a veteran player, wastes no time in adapting and strives to bring stability during this catastrophe. He teams up with his old friend Naotsugu and the petite but fierce Akatsuki, whose favorite food is anpan—and, as she says, anpan is best accompanied by green tea.

- **¼ cup milk**
- **1⅔ cups bread flour**
- **⅓ cup cake flour**
- **¼ cup sugar**
- **1 teaspoon instant dry yeast**
- **½ teaspoon salt**
- **2 large eggs, beaten separately**
- **¼ cup unsalted butter, at room temperature, plus more for greasing**
- **½ cup Anko Sweet Red Bean Paste (recipe follows)**
- **1 tablespoon poppy seeds or black sesame seeds**

1 Combine the milk and ¼ cup water in a heatproof liquid measuring cup and microwave for 30 seconds.

2 Sift and whisk together the bread flour, cake flour, sugar, yeast, and salt in the bowl of a stand mixer. Make a well in the center and add in 1 beaten egg plus the warm milk mixture. Using the dough hook attachment, knead on low speed for 10 minutes, or until the dough is fully combined and smooth.

3 Add in the butter and knead for another 8 to 10 minutes, or until the butter is evenly incorporated and the dough is smooth and elastic. To test if the dough has been kneaded enough, gently stretch a small portion of it between your hands. If it stretches thin enough to see light through, it's good to go, but if it tears easily, it needs to be kneaded some more to develop the gluten.

4 Scrape the dough out of the bowl and shape it into a ball. Lightly butter the mixing bowl and lay the dough back in, smooth side up. Cover the bowl with a sheet of plastic wrap and let the dough rise in a warm place for 1 hour, or until doubled in size. To test if the dough is ready, poke a flour-dusted index finger into the center of the dough. If the hole created stays open, the dough is ready for the next step, but if it closes up, it needs more rising time.

5 Once the dough has risen, punch it down to release air. Remove it from the bowl and press it out to release more air. Fold it like a trifold brochure, then flip it over and fold the edges down to shape it into a ball again.

6 Flatten the ball slightly and divide it into 8 equal wedges. Form each wedge into a ball and place on a large parchment paper–lined baking sheet, 2 inches apart. Cover the baking sheet with plastic wrap and let the dough balls rest for 15 minutes.

7 Flatten each ball into a 4-inch disk, thinner on the edges than the center. Scoop 1 tablespoon of anko into the center of each disc, then fold the dough edges up and over the anko and pinch to seal well. Lay the buns seam side down on the baking sheet. Cover the baking sheet with plastic wrap and let the buns rise in a warm place for 30 minutes, or until doubled in size.

8 When the buns have been rising for 15 minutes, preheat your oven to 400°F. Whisk the second beaten egg with 1 tablespoon of water to make an egg wash and cover until needed. Put the poppy or sesame seeds into a small bowl.

9 When the buns are finished rising, lightly brush the egg wash over each bun. Dip the circle end of a wooden rolling pin or other item with a flat ¾-inch to 1-inch diameter circle into the egg wash, then tap it into the bowl of seeds. Gently stamp the seeds onto the top center of one of the buns. Repeat this "seed-stamping" with each bun. You can also carefully spoon a small amount of seeds onto each bun to create a circle.

10 Slide the baking sheet of decorated buns into the preheated oven and bake for 12 to 15 minutes, or until the buns are a golden brown on top. Remove the baking sheet from the oven and transfer the anpan buns to a cooling rack. Serve warm. If you need to reheat, wrap one anpan in a damp paper towel and microwave for 20 to 30 seconds.

ANKO SWEET RED BEAN PASTE

1 cup red adzuki beans
1 to 1½ cups sugar
Pinch of salt

1 Place the beans in a large bowl and cover with cold water, going 2 inches over the beans. Let the beans soak on the counter overnight.

2 Strain the beans and discard the water. Put the soaked beans into a large pot and cover with water again. Bring to a boil over medium-high heat and cook for 2 minutes. Strain and discard the water again, keeping the beans in the pot.

3 Cover the beans with fresh water, going 2 inches over the beans again, and heat over medium for 1½ to 2 hours, or until the beans are soft and can be easily mashed with the back of a spoon. Skim off any foam that forms during the cooking process and add water as needed if the level goes below the bean line.

4 Strain the liquid into a large bowl and keep the beans in the pot. Strain the liquid a second time through a tea strainer, cheesecloth, or nut milk bag to get the finer bits and add them to the beans in the pot. Keeping the beans whole (or chunky) is the tsubuan version of anko. The smooth version is called koshian: Mash the beans well with the back of a spoon or pulse in a food processor, then press the mixture through a fine-mesh strainer to leave the bean skins behind. Place the bean mixture back in the pot.

5 Stir the sugar and salt into the bean mixture (either tsubuan or koshian) and turn the heat to medium. Cook until the sugar dissolves and the mixture thickens, 10 to 15 minutes, stirring often. Remove the pot from the heat. The bean mixture will thicken more as it cools.

6 Spread the bean mixture onto a baking sheet or large baking dish to cool evenly. Once cool, keep in an airtight container in the refrigerator until ready to use. It'll keep for 2 weeks, or if you freeze it, it can last 2 months.

ANIME FACTS Anpan is the name of the titular character in the famous anime *Anpanman*; he's literally made from anpan! Saitama, better known as One-Punch Man, is a play on the *Anpanman* character. A few of the other characters in *Anpanman* with food-based names are Melonpanna, Karepanman, and Shokupanman. It is said that the creator of *Anpanman*, Takashi Yanase, when faced with starvation during WWII, dreamt often of eating anpan. This eventually led him to create the character Anpanman, which has gone on to be one of the most familiar and beloved characters in Japan.

Anpan features heavily in an episode of the anime *Gintama*, wherein the character spoofs Japanese police dramas and eats so many of the sweet breads that he begins hallucinating.

THIS FOOD ALSO APPEARS IN . . .

- *Gintama*
- *Samurai Flamenco*
- *Yakitate!! Japan*
- *Mr. Tonegawa: Middle Management Blues*
- *Pan de Peace!*
- *Polar Bear Café*
- *Shiki*
- *Anpanman*

SHAKUGAN NO SHANA

MELONPAN

Bun with Cookie Topping

MAKES 8 Fighting the denizens of the Crimson Realm, who feed on human essence, petite, katana-wielding Flame Haze Shana works up quite an appetite for her favorite food, melonpan! This sweet bread contrasts with her initially sour and uncaring personality, but her growing friendship with Torch Yuji Sakai softens her character over time.

1/4 cup milk
1 2/3 cups bread flour
1/3 cup plus 1 1/2 cups cake flour
3/4 cup sugar
1 teaspoon instant dry yeast
1/2 teaspoon plus a pinch salt
2 large eggs, beaten separately
1/2 cup unsalted butter, at room temperature, plus more for greasing
1 teaspoon vanilla extract (optional)
1/4 teaspoon baking powder

1 Combine the milk and 1/4 cup water in a heatproof liquid measuring cup and microwave for 30 seconds.

2 Sift and whisk together the bread flour, 1/3 cup cake flour, 1/4 cup sugar, yeast, and 1/2 teaspoon salt in the bowl of a stand mixer. Make a well in the center and add in 1 beaten egg plus the warm milk mixture. Using the dough hook attachment, knead on low speed for 10 minutes, or until the dough is fully combined and smooth.

3 Add in 1/4 cup butter and knead for another 8 to 10 minutes, or until the butter is evenly incorporated and the dough is smooth and elastic. To test if the dough has been kneaded enough, gently stretch a small portion of it between your hands. If it stretches thin enough to see light through, it's good to go, but if it tears easily, it needs to be kneaded some more to develop the gluten.

4 Scrape the dough out of the bowl and shape it into a ball. Lightly butter a large bowl and place the dough in the bowl, smooth side up. Cover the bowl with a sheet of plastic wrap and let the dough rise in a warm place for 1 hour, until doubled in size. To test if the dough is ready, poke a flour-dusted index finger into the center of the dough. If the hole created stays open, the dough is ready for the next step, but if it closes up, it needs more rising time.

5 Meanwhile, make the cookie dough topping. Cream remaining 1/4 cup butter in a clean, large mixing bowl on medium speed. Mix in 1/4 cup sugar 1 tablespoon at a time until fully combined. Mix in the second egg and the vanilla extract, if using, beating until well incorporated.

6 Sift in 1 1/2 cups of cake flour, the baking powder, and a pinch of salt. Mix on low speed just until a cohesive dough is formed; do not overmix.

7 Scrape the cookie dough out of the bowl, knead a few times, and roll it into a log. Wrap the log in plastic wrap and place it in the refrigerator to chill until needed.

8 Once the bun dough has risen, punch it down to release air. Remove from the bowl and press it out to release more air. Fold it lengthwise, like a trifold brochure, then flip it over and fold the edges down to shape it into a ball again. Flatten the ball slightly and divide into 8 equal wedges. Form each wedge into a ball and place on a large parchment paper–lined baking sheet, 2 inches apart. Cover the baking sheet with plastic wrap and let the dough balls rest for 15 minutes.

9 Put the remaining 1/4 cup sugar in a small bowl. Just before the dough's resting time is up, remove the cookie dough from the refrigerator. Cut the dough log into 8 equal pieces and roll each piece into a ball. Flatten the balls into 4-inch disks.

10 Place 1 cookie dough disk over the top of each dough ball. Smooth the edges of the cookie dough down and around to the bottom of the bun. Next, place the covered bun upside down in the bowl of sugar and roll it around to coat. Lift up the sugared bun and use the back of a butter knife or a bench scraper to make a shallow crosshatching pattern in the cookie dough covering. Place the bun seam side down on the baking sheet and cover with plastic wrap. Repeat this process with the remaining cookie dough and bun dough, placing the buns 2 inches apart on the baking sheet.

11 Once all the buns have been decorated, let them rise in a warm place for 30 minutes, or until doubled in size. After 15 minutes have passed, preheat your oven to 400°F.

12 When the buns are finished rising, slide the baking sheet into the preheated oven and bake for 12 to 15 minutes, or until golden brown. Remove the baking sheet from the oven and transfer the melonpan buns to a cooling rack. Serve warm or at room temperature.

NOTE The dough for this melonpan is the same as the dough for the Anpan (page 98); the only difference is that melonpan has a cookie topping, and anpan has Anko Sweet Red Bean Paste (page 99) in the center.

FOOD FACTS This treat is named melonpan because of the crosshatching design of the cookie topping, not because it has melon or melon flavoring, though you can sometimes find melonpan with melon flavoring or even tinted green. Some shops cut their melonpan open and put whipped cream or soft-serve ice cream inside. Yum!

Melons can be very expensive in Japan, so making an easy-to-grab dessert with a melon-reminiscent pattern is a lighthearted solution.

THIS FOOD ALSO APPEARS IN . . .

- *Free!*
- *Saekano: How to Raise a Boring Girlfriend*
- *Anpanman*
- *Gintama*
- *Samurai Flamenco*
- *Yakitate!! Japan*
- *Mr. Tonegawa: Middle Management Blues*
- *Pan de Peace!*
- *Gabriel Dropout*
- *One Week Friends*
- *Natsume's Book of Friends*
- *Aquarion Evol*
- *Amagami SS*
- *Recorder and Randsell*

GOURMET GIRL GRAFFITI

RINGO AME

Skewered Apples Coated in a Sugar Shell

MAKES 6 After the loss of the grandmother who raised her, kind junior high schooler Ryou Machiko loses her love of cooking, and even food has lost its taste. But when Ryou's cousin Kirin Morino begins staying with her on weekends so they can attend art cram school together, Ryou rediscovers the joy of preparing and sharing meals with loved ones. A special day of cherry-blossom viewing brings excitement, tons of food, new people to meet, new revelations about each other, and Kirin's first taste of candy apple—they can be so pretty!

6 small red apples, such as Fuji or Gala
6 bamboo chopsticks
3 cups sugar
1 teaspoon unseasoned rice vinegar or white vinegar
¼ teaspoon red food coloring

1 Line a large baking sheet with parchment paper. Rinse the apples and dry completely with paper towels. Press a bamboo chopstick into the top of each apple, about half or three-quarters of the way through, just until it's in tightly; do not go all the way through the apple. Wipe any juice away and set the apples on the baking sheet.

2 In a large pot, stir together the sugar, 1½ cups water, and the vinegar. Turn the heat to medium and bring to a boil. Do not stir, but swirl the pot occasionally. Heat for 20 minutes, or until the mixture reaches 300°F on a candy thermometer. Quickly remove the pot from the heat and turn off the stove.

3 Add in the red food coloring and stir with a silicon spatula until the color is evenly distributed. Let the mixture sit for a couple of minutes for the bubbles to subside; tapping the pot on the counter also helps to get rid of bubbles.

4 Tilt the pan and quickly dip and roll each apple in the sugar mixture to give it a thin candy coating, making sure the apple doesn't touch the pot sides while being rotated. Lightly scrape the bottom of the apple on the edge of the pot so excess coating can fall back into the pot. It's all right if the coating doesn't go all the way up to the stem of the apple; it's actually better, because the coating won't come in contact with the apple's juice from the puncture of the chopstick (liquid from the apple will cause the coating to deteriorate). Place each coated apple upright on the parchment paper so the sugar coating can cool and solidify.

5 Serve the coated apples as they are, or place them in cellophane bags tightly closed with a ribbon or twist tie to give as gifts.

NOTE To clean the pot and utensils, fill the pot with water, place the utensils in it, and heat over medium-high heat to dissolve the sugar mixture.

FOOD FACTS *Ringo* means apple, and *ame* denotes sugar and sweets. The hard candy coating is very similar to the Chinese *tanghulu* that often uses haw fruit, which are like little crabapples, but strawberries and grapes are popular, too. You can find these types of candied fruits at Japanese festivals along with mikan ame, which are made with small oranges like mandarins or clementines and can be seen in *Sound! Euphonium*.

Another popular festival food is mizuame (water candy), which is made of starches converted to syrup (like corn syrup) that sits in little depressions on a block of ice. It's served in a small wafer shell, often with fresh fruit segments.

Daigaku imo, meaning university potatoes, are candied Japanese sweet potatoes (satsumaimo) and are often found at school festivals. They consist of deep-fried sweet potato wedges coated in a mixture of sugar, syrup, and soy sauce, then sprinkled with black sesame seeds.

THIS FOOD ALSO APPEARS IN . . .

- *Haganai: I Don't Have Many Friends*
- *Kill Me Baby*
- *Upotte!!*
- *Ground Control to Psychoelectric Girl*
- *Guilty Crown*
- *Wolf Girl & Black Prince*
- *The Quintessential Quintuplets*
- *Iroduku: The World in Colors*
- *My Sweet Tyrant*
- *Sengoku Collection*
- *Hayate the Combat Butler! Heaven is a Place on Earth*
- *Wataten!: An Angel Flew Down to Me*
- *Alice in Borderland*

MAGICAL ANGEL CREAMY MAMI

CREPES

SERVES 4 Energetic ten-year-old Yuu Morisawa discovers an alien ship and is granted magical powers for a year, along with the ability to transform into a sixteen-year-old as a disguise. One day while transformed, Yuu is scouted by a music company and becomes an instant idol sensation, taking the name "Creamy" from her parents' "Creamy Crepes" shop.

½ cup all-purpose flour

2 tablespoons sugar

Pinch of salt

1 large egg, at room temperature

¾ cup milk, at room temperature

1 tablespoon unsalted butter, melted, plus more for greasing the pan

FOR THE WHIPPED CREAM

1 cup heavy whipping cream, chilled

2 tablespoons powdered sugar

Pinch of cream of tartar (optional)

1 Sift the flour, sugar, and salt into a medium bowl. In a separate bowl, whisk the egg, then whisk in the milk and the melted butter. Make a well in the center of the flour mixture and pour in half of the milk mixture, whisking as you do so. Once a smooth paste is formed, whisk in the rest of the liquid. Cover the bowl with plastic wrap and let sit on the counter for 30 minutes.

2 Meanwhile, make the whipped cream: Place a large mixing bowl and whisk attachment into the freezer for at least 15 minutes. Remove from the freezer, pour in the cream, sift in the powdered sugar, and whisk at medium speed until stiff peaks form. Adding in a pinch of cream of tartar along with the sugar will help the whipped cream stabilize for longer, but it isn't necessary if you'll be using the cream right away.

3 Stir the batter, then strain it through a fine-mesh strainer into a liquid measuring cup. Heat a 10-inch skillet over medium heat and brush with butter once it's hot. Lift the pan with one hand and pour ¼ cup of batter into the pan with the other hand while swirling the pan to spread the batter evenly across the bottom. Cook for 40 seconds, or until the batter is set on the top. Use a large spatula to gently turn the crepe over to cook for another 15 seconds, then slide the crepe onto a large plate. Re-butter the pan, stir the batter, and repeat the process until all of the batter is used up, stacking the crepes as you go.

NOTE Traditional crepes, originally from France, are often served folded on a plate with toppings such as butter, sugar, cinnamon, fresh fruit or preserves, or whipped cream. But in the colorful Harajuku district in Shibuya, Japan, crepes rolled into cones are popular with both traditional fillings as well as more creative ones, such as cheesecake, ice cream, Purin (page 114), crème brûlée, custard, nuts, brownies, wafers and cookies, macarons, Dango (page 118)—there are so many possibilities!

ANIME FACTS *Creamy Mami* wasn't the first magical girl (that honor belongs to 1966's *Sally the Witch*), but she set the genre alight starting in 1983 and inspired anime like *Persia the Magic Fairy*, *Magical Emi*, *Pastel Yumi*, and *Fancy Lala*. *Mami* was also the pioneer of combining anime with up-and-coming real-life idol singers, and was followed by anime such as *Legendary Idol Eriko* and *Idol Angel Yokoso Yoko*.

THIS FOOD ALSO APPEARS IN . . .

- *Toradora!*
- *Bungo Stray Dogs*
- *Code Geass*
- *Is the Order a Rabbit?*
- *A Certain Scientific Railgun*
- *Is It Wrong to Try to Pick Up Girls in a Dungeon?*
- *Nyaruko: Crawling with Love!*
- *Comic Girls*
- *Clannad*
- *Dog Days*
- *Place to Place*
- *X/1999*
- *Baka and Test: Summon the Beasts*
- *Amagami SS*

REVOLUTIONARY GIRL UTENA

KAKIGORI

Shaved Ice with Flavored Syrup

SERVES 1 Inspired by the noble character of a prince who gave her a rose signet ring when she was younger, Utena Tenjou is determined to become a prince herself one day. As a teenager, she begins attending the prestigious Ohtori Academy, where she gets caught up in duels with various student council members, each owning a similar signet ring and all desiring the hand of the "Rose Bride," Anthy Himemiya. After one hard battle, Anthy brings Utena a cool and refreshing kakigori to revive her.

1 cup sugar
1 cup chopped strawberries
½ teaspoon plus ¼ cup lemon juice
Peel from ½ lemon
Pinch of saffron threads or yellow food coloring (optional)
8 ounces ice

1 In a medium pot over medium heat, stir together ½ cup of the sugar, the strawberries, and ½ teaspoon lemon juice. Bring the mixture to a boil, stirring often, and continue to cook for 3 minutes. Remove from the heat and strain through a fine-mesh strainer into a cup. You can save the strawberry pulp for a topping, if you'd like. Cool the syrup to room temperature, then place it in the refrigerator to fully chill, about 30 minutes.

2 In a medium pot over medium heat, stir together the remaining ½ cup of sugar, ¼ cup lemon juice, and the lemon peel. Bring to a boil and cook for 3 minutes. Strain the mixture through a fine-mesh strainer into a cup and let cool to room temperature before placing it in the refrigerator to fully chill. To achieve a more vibrant yellow color, stir in the saffron threads or a couple of drops of yellow food coloring.

3 Using a kakigori machine, shave the ice into a bowl, gently compacting the shaved ice with a cold spoon or spatula as you go, until you get a nice mound. Alternatively, put the ice in a blender or food processor and pulse until the ice is fluffy (but this may dull the blades of your machine). Another method is to use a sharp knife on a premade block of ice, though you'll have to be mindful of your fingers! To make an ice block, completely freeze 3 cups of water in a freezer-safe container. Let the block sit out for 5 to 10 minutes, then remove it from the container and stand it on its side on a cutting board. Hold the ice steady with a pot holder while you use the knife to shave the side of the ice.

4 Pour the chilled strawberry syrup in a thin, zigzagging stream over the left side of the kakigori, then pour the chilled lemon syrup over the right side. Serve immediately with a spoon.

NOTES To make matcha syrup, sift 1 tablespoon of culinary-grade matcha powder with ½ cup sugar into a small bowl and whisk in ½ cup boiling water, a little at a time, until the matcha and sugar have dissolved.

For a natural blue syrup, combine ½ cup sugar and ½ cup boiling water with 5 dried butterfly pea flowers, let the sugar dissolve and the flowers steep until the liquid is a vibrant blue, then remove the flowers. Chill the syrups before using as above.

FOOD FACTS There are many different syrup flavors for kakigori, such as blue Hawaiian—seen in *Blast of Tempest* and *Yuri Bear Storm*—cherry, melon, grape, plum, and matcha tea, as seen in *Someday's Dreamers* and *Non Non Biyori*.

There is a type of matcha kakigori called ujikintoki kakigori, seen in *Yuuna and the Haunted Hot Springs* and *Sakura Quest*, which includes Tsubuan Anko (page 99), Dango (page 118), drizzled condensed milk, and sometimes Matcha Ice Cream (page 132). Ujikintoki references Uji in Kyoto, where high-quality matcha is produced, and Sakata no Kintoki, a figure from folklore who was said to have ruddy skin, the red beans on ujikintoki kakigori being an allusion to that. Sakata no Kintoki was originally named Kintaro, meaning "golden boy," but he changed his name when he became a follower of samurai Minamoto no Yorimitsu, who in reality did have a loyal warrior named Sakata Kintoki.

Another style of kakigori is shirokuma, which means "white bear," or "polar bear," more specifically. This version is often garnished with fresh fruit to look like a cute polar bear face. Other fun renditions seen in anime are the mango kakigori in *Cheer Boys!!*, with sunflower seeds sprinkled on top, and the coffee kakigori from *The Disastrous Life of Saiki K.*, with cubes of Coffee Jelly (page 124).

CULTURE FACTS Kakigori is said to date back to the eleventh century in Japan and was a luxury food only available to nobles and royalty. Natural ice blocks were saved from winter in special storehouses for use in the summer, and a knife was used to shave the ice into a bowl. It wasn't until the mid-1800s, with the invention of the ice maker, that ice became more widely available to the public year-round. In the early 1900s, an ice-shaving machine was invented, and kakigori became available to everyone. You can find variously priced kakigori machines online.

Kakigori flourishes in the summertime and can be found at cafés, festivals, and street stalls all over Japan. The texture is what sets it apart from other types of shaved ice desserts, as kakigori is shaved in a way that makes it soft and fluffy, like freshly fallen snow.

 THIS FOOD ALSO APPEARS IN . . .

- *Barakamon*
- *Dropkick on My Devil!*
- *Minky Momo: The Bridge Over Dreams*
- *Nekopara*
- *Yowamushi Pedal: Glory Line*
- *A Place Further than the Universe*
- *Scared Riders Xechs*
- *RobiHachi*
- *Prince of Stride: Alternative*
- *Urusei Yatsura*
- *Sound! Euphonium!*
- *Ms. Koizumi Loves Ramen Noodles*
- *Today's Menu for the Emiya Family*
- *Yuri Bear Storm*
- *Lagrange: The Flower of Rin-ne*
- *A Certain Scientific Railgun*
- *Someday's Dreamers*
- *Sakura Quest*
- *Cheer Boys!!*
- *Case Closed*

FOUR

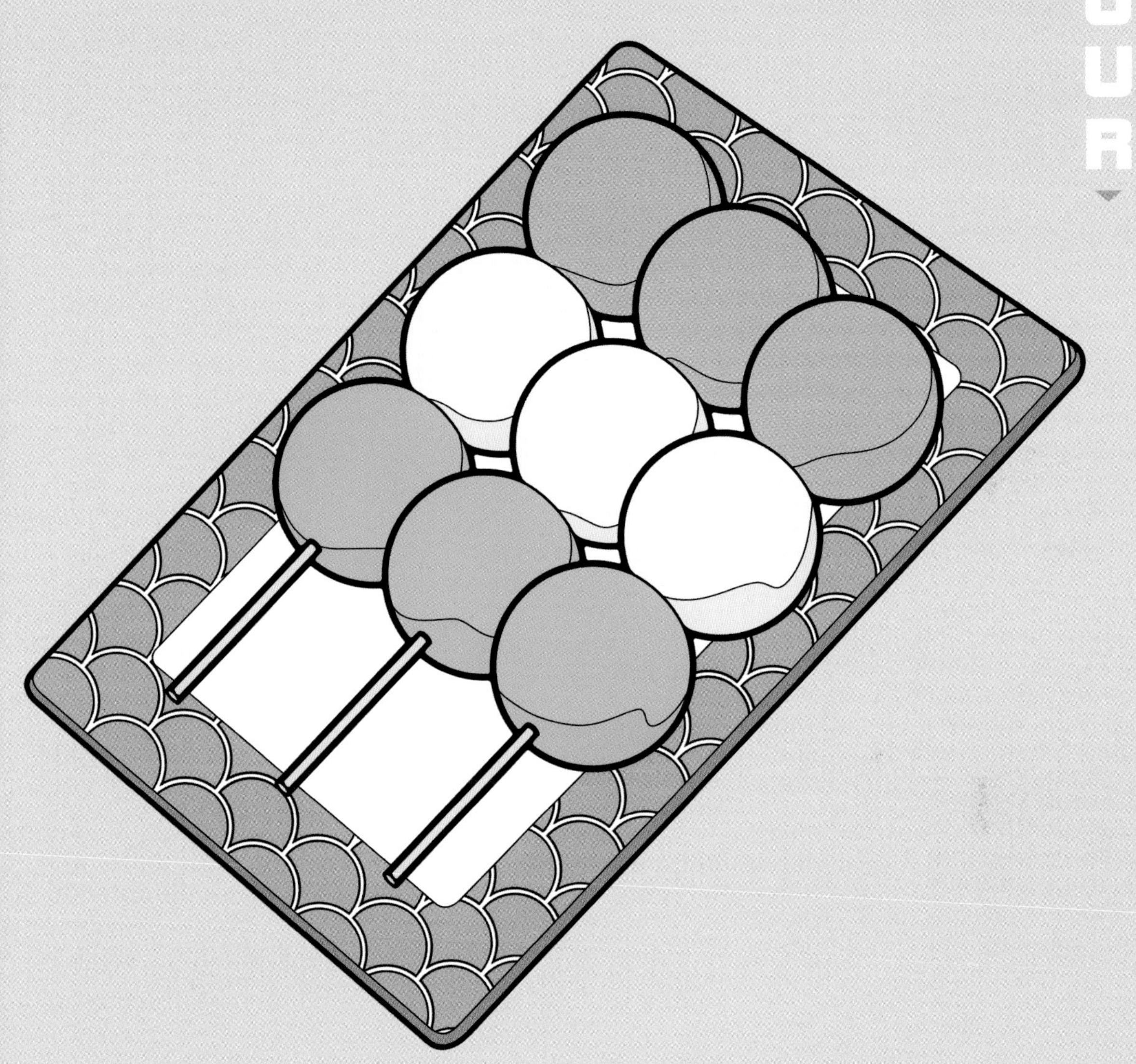

DRINKS & DESSERTS

THE MELANCHOLY OF HARUHI SUZUMIYA

MELON CREAM SODA

Soda with Melon Syrup and Ice Cream

SERVES 1 Intense and confident, Haruhi Suzumiya is convinced that there's more to this mundane world than meets the eye, and is bound and determined to prove it! She commandeers the literary club room along with the taciturn Yuki Nagano (who just happens to be in the room) and, together with a small group of intriguing fellow students, forms the SOS Brigade to seek out the supernatural. They often meet up at the local coffee shop, where Yuki regularly orders melon cream sodas.

1/4 large honeydew melon
1 cup sugar
Bright green food coloring
Yellow food coloring (optional)
2 cups carbonated water
1 scoop vanilla ice cream
1 fresh or maraschino cherry (optional)

1 Cut the rind from the melon and chop the interior into 1/2-inch chunks, discarding any seeds. Place the melon chunks and 1/4 cup water in a standing blender and blend on high speed until smooth. Strain the mixture into a glass measuring cup or pitcher through a cheesecloth or nut milk bag to remove the pulp, repeating the straining process as needed to get the most juice and the least pulp.

2 Combine 1 cup water with the sugar in a medium pot over medium-low heat and cook just until the sugar is dissolved completely. Remove from the heat and let cool. This is the simple syrup.

3 Once the simple syrup is cool, combine 3/4 cup with the melon liquid. Whisk in several drops of green food coloring until the liquid is a bright, uniform color, adding in a couple of yellow drops if desired to make the color more vibrant.

4 Stir the melon syrup into the carbonated water and add more simple syrup and/or more carbonated water according to your taste. Fill a tall glass with ice cubes up to 1 inch from the top and pour in the melon soda. Place the scoop of ice cream on top and garnish with a cherry, if desired. Serve with a straw and a long spoon.

FOOD FACTS Melon can be very expensive in Japan, so you'll often find sweet foods and drinks with melon flavoring at a fraction of the price. Melon cream soda is to Japan what a root beer float is to America. In anime, you can find melon soda topped with ice cream, as in this recipe, or with whipped cream, or simply plain.

CULTURE FACTS The Dream Coffee Shop in *The Melancholy of Haruhi Suzumiya* was inspired by the real-life Café Dream in the city of Nishinomiya, Hyogo Prefecture, frequented by the author of the original Haruhi Suzumiya novel series, Nagaru Tanigawa. Melon cream soda wasn't initially on the café's menu but was added after it was requested by many anime fans. The café even has a special notebook that fans can sign when they visit. Café Dream changed location in 2017, but didn't move too far from the original spot.

THIS DRINK ALSO APPEARS IN . . .

- *Sailor Moon*
- *Amnesia*
- *Penguin Highway*
- *Cardcaptor Sakura*
- *Maid-Sama!*
- *Aikatsu Stars!*
- *When Supernatural Battles Became Commonplace*
- *Servant x Service*
- *The Case Files of Jeweler Richard*
- *Restaurant to Another World*
- *Urara Meirocho*
- *B-Project*
- *Your Lie in April*
- *Seiren*
- *My First Girlfriend Is a Gal*
- *Domestic Girlfriend*

ROYAL MILK TEA

Black Tea Simmered with Milk

SERVES 1 Blessed with a brilliant mind and cursed with a beautiful face, jeweler Richard Ranasinghe de Vulpian sets up shop in Japan and hires college student Seigi Nakata as his part-time assistant after Seigi comes to his rescue one night. Seigi learns not just the monetary value of gemstones but also their value as precious items of the heart. He also learns that Richard has a sweet tooth, and that his favorite drink—milk tea—must be made just so.

2 teaspoons loose-leaf black tea

½ cup milk (non-dairy milk is fine)

2 teaspoons to 1 tablespoon sugar

1 Bring ½ cup water to a boil in a medium pot over medium-high heat. Stir in the loose-leaf tea and reduce the heat to medium-low. Let the tea simmer for 2 minutes.

2 Pour the milk into the pot. When it starts to gently steam, remove the pot from the heat. Add the sugar, cover the pot, and let sit undisturbed for 5 minutes. You can add more or less sugar to taste.

3 Uncover the pot and strain the milk tea through a tea strainer or fine-mesh strainer into a cup to serve hot. If you'd like chilled milk tea, strain it into a cup and let it come to room temperature. You can add ice cubes at this point, or chill in the refrigerator before serving. Feel free to add more milk to your liking.

NOTES Richard loves sweet things, but if you're not too keen, you can omit the sugar. If you're serving this to someone else, you can place a little pot of sugar, honey, or agave nectar on the side so that they can sweeten the milk tea to their liking.

To make white chocolate milk tea, as seen in *Bonjour Sweet Love Patisserie*, simply prepare a pot of royal milk tea and after straining it into a cup, stir ⅓ to ½ cup finely chopped white chocolate into the still hot liquid. Stir until the chocolate is incorporated and melted (the smaller the pieces, the easier and quicker they will melt).

HONEY GINGER MILK

Do you remember that scene in *Ponyo* when the primordial storm is raging outside and Ponyo and Sosuke are bundled up all cozy inside? Sosuke's mom brings them two steaming cups of a pale drink and adds heaping spoonfuls of golden honey. We're not told what the drink is, but perhaps it's milk tea? It could simply be warm milk or, as in *Yuri Bear Storm*, it could even be ginger milk!

2 ½ cups milk (non-dairy milk is fine here)

1 (1-inch) piece fresh ginger, finely grated

Honey, for serving

1 In a medium pot over medium heat, warm the milk until scalding—it should be steaming with tiny bubbles formed. Reduce the heat to low for a steady simmer and stir in the ginger. Cook for 8 minutes, then strain through a fine-mesh strainer.

2 Stir in honey, according to your taste.

FOOD FACTS In Japan, milk tea is sometimes referred to as Hokkaido milk tea because Hokkaido is the major farming and milk-producing region in Japan. "Royal Milk Tea" was coined by the Lipton tea company in the 1950s. It is such a popular beverage in Japan that many varieties are featured throughout the year based on seasonal flavors. You can even get cans of it in vending machines all over Japan!

Milk tea is often used in boba tea (also known as bubble or tapioca pearl tea), and you can see it in anime such as *Scum's Wish* and *Shin Atashinchi*.

THIS TEA IS ALSO FOUND IN . . .

- *Magical Angel Creamy Mami*
- *Free! Dive to the Future*
- *Engaged to the Unidentified*
- *Hi Score Girl*
- *Bonjour Sweet Love Patisserie*
- *Scum's Wish*
- *Shin Atashinchi*

夜

NORAGAMI

GREEN TEA

SERVES 1 Stray god Yato is trying to make a name for himself but is severely down on his luck. With no dedicated shrine or followers to pay their respects, he does odd jobs, makes deliveries, and grants wishes for a mere five yen apiece. His luck starts to change when he is (unnecessarily) saved from being hit by a bus by junior high schooler Hiyori Iki.

- **1 teaspoon loose-leaf green tea, such as karigane, kuchika, or sencha**
- **1 cup water, preferably purified or filtered water (not distilled)**
- **Honey or other sweetener, to taste (optional)**

1 Place the tea leaves in a large tea infuser, in the strainer basket of a teapot, or in a teapot with a sasame filter (see Notes below).

2 In a small pot over medium heat, bring 1 cup of water to 165°F to 170°F. Do not boil.

3 If using a tea infuser sitting in your cup, pour the hot water directly from the pot into your cup. If using a teapot, pour the hot water first into your teacup to warm the cup, then pour the water from the cup into the teapot over the tea leaves.

4 Steep the tea leaves for up to 1 minute if using karigane or kuchika, and up to 2 minutes for sencha. Any longer will impart a bitter and astringent taste.

5 If the tea leaves are in an infuser, remove it from the tea. If using a teapot, pour the tea into your teacup. Add sweetener to taste, if desired.

6 If you're serving more than one person, heat another cup of water as before. If you used an infuser, place it in a second cup and continue as before. If using a teapot, keep the leaves in the pot and pour the hot water over them as before.

7 If not brewing another cup of tea immediately or within 1½ hours, lay the used leaves out in a single layer on paper towels to dry in a dark place and use within 12 hours.

NOTES If using gyokuro tea, use 1 heaping teaspoon of tea leaves, heat the water to 135°F, and steep the leaves for 1½ to 2 minutes.

A Japanese teapot is called a kyusu and can contain different types of strainers. The type of strainer that is more likely to let a twig get through is the sasame style, which is not made of fine mesh like other strainers but is a series of holes on the inside of the teapot directly leading to the spout.

FOOD FACTS There are many types of Japanese green tea, but they are all from the *Camellia sinensis* species of plant, also simply known as the tea plant. The way that the plant is grown, harvested, and processed and the degree of oxidation give each tea a different flavor and aroma, either subtle or substantial. Sencha is the most commonly available type of green tea. Bancha is a less flavorful version of sencha and is less expensive because of it. Gyokuro is made from leaves that have been grown in shade and contains more L-theanine. Karigane and kuchika (or bocha), also known as twig tea, are made of the stem and twig bits of the tea plant—the former from gyokuro and high-grade sencha, and the latter from bancha and lower-grade sencha. These are the teas most likely to gift a little twig to your cup, especially if used in a kyusu with a sasame strainer spout. Hojicha is made from roasted tea leaves and is good in Chazuke (page 33). Genmaicha has sencha or bancha as its base and contains roasted rice.

CULTURE FACTS Finding a tea twig floating upright in your tea is considered good luck. This rare occurrence is called *chabashira*, which means "tea pillar." It's said that a long time ago, a tea merchant invented the idea in order to sell the twiggy bits of tea that weren't popular at the time. In anime, chabashira can also be seen as foreshadowing, so keep an eye out for it!

THIS DRINK ALSO APPEARS IN . . .

- *Bungo Stray Dogs*
- *K: Missing Kings*
- *Love Live! Sunshine!!*
- *Amagami SS*
- *Food Wars!*
- *In Another World with My Smartphone*
- *The Great Passage*
- *Natsume's Book of Friends*
- *Hina Logic—from Luck & Logic*
- *Glasslip*
- *Cardcaptor Sakura: Clear Card*

THE GIRL WHO LEAPT THROUGH TIME

PURIN

Caramel Custard

SERVES 4 Would you go back in time to rescue a delicious treat from being eaten by your sister? After tripping over a strange, small object at school and almost being run over by a train on her way home, Makoto Konno gains the ability to time-leap. She uses this power for small and selfish reasons—like punctuality, karaoke, good grades, and savoring her purin—but as the past and present, and the lives of those she cares about, get tangled up from all of the leaping, she has to take responsibility.

Butter, for greasing
1/2 cup sugar
1 tablespoon very hot water, plus more for baking
2 large eggs, plus 2 egg yolks, at room temperature
1 1/2 cups milk, at room temperature
1/4 cup heavy cream
1 teaspoon vanilla extract

1 Butter 4 medium-size ramekins, custard or pudding molds, or other heatproof cups.

2 In a small pot, briefly stir together 1/4 cup of sugar with 2 tablespoons of water. Place on the stove over medium heat; do not stir anymore. Heat until the sugar dissolves and the mixture turns a deep golden brown—the darker it gets, the more bitter it will taste, so heat to your preference. Remove from the stove and immediately pour in the 1 tablespoon hot water. The mixture will sizzle and spit. Swirl it around while holding the pot handle, then pour the liquid evenly into the prepared cups.

3 In a large bowl, whisk the eggs and egg yolks well so the whites are completely broken up, but try not to lift your whisk to avoid adding too much air into the mixture. Place a clean, small pot on the stove over medium heat and add the milk, remaining 1/2 cup sugar, and vanilla. Stir occasionally and heat just until the sugar is dissolved; do not boil.

4 In small, gradual amounts, whisk the milk mixture into the beaten eggs. Slowly pour the mixture through a fine-mesh strainer into a medium bowl, then strain it again from the bowl to a liquid measuring cup or other cup with a spout. Divide the mixture equally into the prepared cups by pouring it over the back of a spoon so that the mixture slides slowly down the sides and avoids creating bubbles. Leave at least 1/2 inch of space at the top of each cup. If there are any bubbles on top, skim them off with a spoon.

5 Place the cups in a baking dish and pour very hot water into the dish until the water reaches halfway up the cups. Cover with aluminum foil and slide the dish into the oven to bake for 30 minutes, or until the purin is set and the tops jiggle when the cups are tapped. Remove from the oven and use pot holders to remove the purin cups from the dish. Place the cups on a flat kitchen towel to cool to room temperature, and then cover the cups with plastic wrap and place them in the refrigerator to chill for at least 2 hours.

6 To serve, run the thin blade of a knife along the inside edge of the purin cups, then invert the cups onto a serving dish; the caramel sugar syrup will run down the sides.

FOOD FACTS *Purin* is the Japanese phonetic pronunciation of "pudding," but this dessert is a custard pudding or caramel custard akin to crème caramel or flan.

Purin is often seen in anime in little cups from the konbini or convenience store, but can also be found inverted on a dessert plate with the caramel side facing up like in this recipe. Sometimes you'll see it with whipped cream (page 124) or ice cream and fruit "à la mode" style, like in *Restaurant to Another World*, *WWW.WAGNARIA!!*, and *THE IDOLM@STER*, or even atop a parfait like in *K-On!*. In *The Case Files of Jeweler Richard*, there's special purin made using Okinawan black sugar, which is unrefined and has a bit of a salted caramel taste. If you can get this unique sugar, use it in place of the granulated sugar in the syrup, or try muscovado or dark brown sugar. In *Okko's Inn* and *KiraKira PreCure a la Mode*, you'll see black sesame (kuro goma) purin, which incorporates a paste made from toasted black sesame seeds that turns the purin a striking gray.

ANIME FACTS *The Girl Who Leapt Through Time*, directed by Mamoru Hosoda (*Summer Wars*, *Wolf Children*, *Mirai*, etc.), is both an adaptation and a loose sequel to the story of the same name by Yasutaka Tsutsui, originally serialized in Japan from 1965 to 1966 and published in novel form in 1967. The story focuses on Kazuko Yoshiyama (Makoto's art-restoring aunt in the anime), a student who obtains the ability to time travel in short leaps. Mishaps, self-discovery, and romance ensue. In the anime, Kazuko alludes to this experience, but if you're unaware of the source material, it might leave you guessing. Tsutsui's story was also adapted into live-action films in 1983 and 1997, with a sequel in 2010, as well as live-action TV series in 1972, 1994, and 2016.

THIS FOOD ALSO APPEARS IN . . .

- *Nanana's Buried Treasure*
- *Okko's Inn*
- *A Place Further Than the Universe*
- *Assassination Classroom*
- *Natsume's Book of Friends*
- *March Comes in Like a Lion*
- *Layton Mystery Detective Agency: Katri's Puzzle Solving Files*
- *Crayon Shin-chan*
- *Wataten!: An Angel Flew Down to Me*
- *Maison Ikkoku*
- *JoJo's Bizarre Adventure: Diamond Is Unbreakable*
- *Love Is Like a Cocktail*
- *Toriko*
- *Convenience Store Boy Friends*
- *The Moment You Fall in Love*
- *Tsugumomo*
- *Sakura Quest*
- *World End*
- *Boy Maid*
- *Skip Beat*
- *Sengoku Paradise*
- *Strawberry Panic*
- *KiraKira PreCure a la Mode*
- *WWW .WAGNARIA!!*
- *Restaurant to Another World*

TAMAKO MARKET

MOCHI

Soft Sweet Rice Ball

MAKES 8 Tamako Kitashirakawa's life is filled with mochi. Her family runs a mochi shop, she acquires a strange bird named Dera Mochimazzi who loves to eat mochi, and even her best childhood friend (whose family also runs a mochi shop) is named Mochizo! As Tamako goes about her daily life, comedy and romance ensue, all wrapped in mochi-mochi softness.

½ cup mochiko or shiratamako short-grain rice flour

⅓ cup sugar

Cornstarch or potato starch, for dusting

1 In a medium microwave-safe bowl, stir together the rice flour and ½ cup water to make a smooth paste, then stir in the sugar until well combined. Cover the bowl with plastic wrap and microwave for 1 minute. Use a potholder to remove the bowl from the microwave and stir the mixture with a wet spatula, folding it over several times. Cover the bowl with plastic wrap again and microwave for another minute. Stir and fold again with a wet spatula. The mochi will be very hot and incredibly sticky.

2 Dust a flat work surface generously with starch, and dust your hands as well. Scoop the mochi mixture onto the starch-dusted work surface, then fold it into a log, being careful as you handle it. Dust a knife or bench scraper with starch and cut the log into 8 equal segments. Fold each segment into a ball, pinching the edges together underneath and rolling the ball in your hand to round it out, re-dusting your hands with starch as needed. The mochi is now ready to serve.

NOTES Please don't try to eat a mochi all at once, as the consistency makes it possible to get stuck in your throat.

Daifuku mochi is mochi wrapped around a filling, often seen in anime containing anko red bean paste. To make daifuku mochi, you will need ½ cup Anko Red Bean Paste (page 99; either tsubuan or koshian is fine). Make the mochi recipe above, but flatten the mochi segments, place a tablespoon ball of anko in the center, fold the mochi around the anko, and pinch the mochi closed.

In *Tamako Market* we see kuromame daifuku mochi, also called mame mochi or mame daifuku, which contains boiled kuromame, or black soybeans. This type of mochi represents great luck and good health. To make this variation, fold boiled black soybeans or azuki beans into freshly made mochi dough, then divide the dough and fill with anko as when making regular daifuku.

Ichigo daifuku mochi is plain mochi wrapped around anko with a fresh strawberry inside. This type is seen in *Listen to Me, Girls, I'm Your Father!*, *Super Lovers*, and many other anime. To make ichigo daifuku mochi, you'll need ½ cup of koshian anko and 8 fresh strawberries. Rinse the strawberries, pat them dry, and remove their stems. Wrap 1 tablespoon of anko around each strawberry, leaving the strawberry tip pointing up. Flatten out the mochi segments and fold and seal one around each anko-covered strawberry. Another version of ichigo daifuku, as seen in *KiraKira PreCure a la Mode*, uses kitchen shears to cut an opening in regular daifuku mochi (the cut looks like a mouth) where a strawberry is then snuggled.

For ice cream mochi, known as yukimi daifuku mochi or daifuku aisu, place eight 1-tablespoon scoops of your choice of ice cream (like matcha, page 132) in a plastic wrap-lined mini muffin tin and refreeze for at least 1 hour. Flatten fresh mochi segments into discs and wrap one each around the ice cream balls, then wrap each ice cream mochi in plastic wrap. Place the mochi in the freezer for at least 3 hours, then let them sit on the counter for 5 minutes before serving.

You can also dip pieces of mochi in water and then toss them in a mixture of two parts kinako (powdered roasted soybeans) to one part granulated sugar to make kinako mochi. Kuromitsu syrup (page 123) is delicious drizzled over this.

CULTURE FACTS Historically, and even still today, to celebrate the New Year, mochi is made by pounding steamed short-grain rice in a large pestle with a special mortar hammer called a surikogi. One person swings the hammer while another person quickly turns the pounded mochi. The process takes great teamwork and trust. You can see this process in anime such as *Elegant Yokai Apartment Life* and *Place to Place*. A Japanese folktale tells of a rabbit pounding mochi on the moon. Sailor Moon's name, Usagi Tsukino, is an allusion to tsuki no usagi, which means "moon rabbit."

In lieu of pounding rice to make mochi (which is very labor-intensive), home cooks use mochigome rice flour, as in the recipe above. Another option uses sweet glutinous rice that is rinsed, soaked, and cooked as with regular rice (page 52), and then the hot rice is placed in the bowl of a stand mixer and kneaded on medium speed for 20 minutes, or until smooth and sticky.

As you can see, there are many different variations of mochi made for many different cultural purposes!

- **Hishimochi** is a square of layered mochi in the same colors as Hanami Dango (page 118)—pink, white, and green—and is made for Hinamatsuri, also known as the Doll Festival or Girls' Day.
- **Kusa mochi**, meaning "grass mochi," is deep green thanks to the addition of mugwort powder, known as yomogi, which has medicinal properties.
- **Kagami Mochi**, which means "mirror mochi," is displayed for the new year and consists of two stacked white mochi, a smaller one atop a larger one, with a small orange mochi on

top. Mochi is also added to the traditional New Year's soups Ozoni and Zenzai.

- **Kashiwa Mochi** is anko-filled white mochi wrapped in an oak leaf and eaten on Children's Day (also known as Boys' Day).
- **Sakura Mochi** celebrates both *sakura* (cherry blossom) season and Hinamatsuri and is made of pink-tinted mochi with visible mochigome grains that's filled with anko and wrapped in a pickled sakura leaf.
- To celebrate Higan during the spring and autumn equinoxes, **botamochi** and **ohagi** are made with lightly pounded mochigome that's typically wrapped in anko, but can also be coated in kinako, walnut, or sesame.
- Thoroughly dried mochi can be turned into **okaki**, also called kakimochi or agemochi, when fried. A popular, smaller version of okaki is called arare, and was the inspiration for Akira Toriyama's robot character Arale Norimaki, whose last name refers to the type of arare wrapped with nori seaweed.

THIS FOOD ALSO APPEARS IN . . .

- *Natsume's Book of Friends*
- *Vampire Princess Miyu*
- *Kochoki: Wakaki Nobunaga*
- *Yuri!!! on Ice*
- *Elegant Yokai Apartment Life*
- *Tamako Market*
- *Yotsuiro Biyori*
- *Place to Place*

CLANNAD

HANAMI DANGO

Tricolored Rice Flour Dumplings

MAKES 6 DUMPLINGS Tomoya Okazaki's mother passed away when he was young, and his father turned to gambling and drink, pushing Tomoya toward a delinquent lifestyle. In his last year of high school, however, he meets the soft-spoken Nagisa Furukawa, an ailing fan of The Big Dango Family mascot who dreams of joining the school drama club. Tomoya agrees to help Nagisa restart the club, making and helping many friends and learning the true meaning of family in the process.

- **1/2 cup shiratamako or mochiko glutinous rice flour**
- **1/4 cup plus a dash hot water**
- **1/2 cup joshinko or other non-glutinous rice flour**
- **1 tablespoon sugar**
- **1/4 to 1/2 teaspoon mugwort powder or 1/2 teaspoon matcha powder**
- **Red food coloring**
- **Wooden skewers, for serving**

1 Set a medium pot filled three-quarters with water to boil over medium-high heat.

2 In a medium bowl, stir together the shiratamako and hot water until the rice flour is dissolved. Add the joshinko and sugar and stir until well combined. Gradually stir in small amounts of water at a time (up to another 1/4 cup) until the texture of the dough is soft like an earlobe.

3 Knead the dough to make it very smooth and divide into 3 equal segments, putting a little rice flour on your hands if needed. Place the segments in separate small bowls and cover with plastic wrap so the dough won't dry out.

4 Place the mugwort or matcha powder in a small bowl and add a dash of hot water. Mix the water and powder thoroughly to create a paste, adding more water in tiny amounts if needed. Using a toothpick, add small amounts of the paste to one of the bowls of dough, kneading it until you get a smooth, light green color. The color will darken slightly when boiled. You can make it as dark or light as you'd like. Wash your hands well so as not to transfer color to the other dough sections.

5 Add one drop of red food coloring to one of the other bowls of dough and knead well to incorporate it evenly. Add another drop if you'd like a darker shade, again keeping in mind that the color with deepen when boiling. Wash your hands again to make sure you don't have any red coloring on them.

6 Fill a large bowl halfway with cold water and add in several ice cubes to create an ice bath.

7 Remove the plain dough from its bowl, roll it into a log, and divide into 6 equal pieces. Roll each piece into a ball and lower the balls into the boiling pot of water. Once they float to the top, let them cook for an additional 2 minutes. Scoop them out with a slotted spoon and immediately place in the ice bath.

8 Next, roll the pink dough into a log and divide into 6 equal pieces. Roll these pieces into balls and place them in the boiling water and cook just like the white dango, placing them in the ice bath afterward. Repeat this process with the green dough. Turn off the heat when done and discard the water.

9 Once all of the dango are cooked and cooled in the ice bath, thread them on small bamboo skewers in the pattern of green on the bottom, white in the middle, and pink on the top, and serve.

FOOD FACTS An unskewered dango is often made with an indentation when added to other desserts such as Anmitsu (page 123), Parfait (page 128), and Kakigori (page 104). These dango are called shiratama dango because traditionally they are made with shiratamako flour (which gives the best dango texture).

CULTURE FACTS *Hanami*, meaning "flower viewing," is a special time of year in Japan that takes place during spring to celebrate the blossoming pink *sakura* (cherry) and white *ume* (plum) trees. Hanami dango is a common treat during this time, as its colors reflect those of the season and represent the sentiments of blooming, purity, and growth. These chewy sweets are also called sanshoku dango because of the three (san) colors. Hanami dango shares the colors and symbolism of hishi mochi, which is served on March 3, Hinamatsuri (Dolls' Day or Girls' Day).

ANIME FACTS Did you know Usagi Tsukino, aka Sailor Moon, sports what's known as an odango hairstyle, named after the soft round dango? In the English releases of *Sailor Moon*, though, instead of being called *odango atama* ("dango head"), she's called meatball or bun head!

THIS FOOD ALSO APPEARS IN . . .

- *Suite PreCure*
- *Naruto: Shippuden*
- *Yotsuiro Biyori*
- *Touken Ranbu: Hanamaru*
- *Katanagatari*
- *Urara Meirocho*
- *Is the Order a Rabbit?*

HIMOUTO! UMARU-CHAN

VALENTINE CHOCOLATES

MAKES 10 TO 20 CHOCOLATES Umaru Doma is friendly and pretty, gets good grades, and is good at sports; she's an all-rounder at school. But at home? Oh boy, is she a different person! She snacks on junk food, plays video games, and watches anime until the wee hours of the morning. She depends heavily on her older brother, Taihei, to take care of her. One Valentine's Day, their shy neighbor Ebina invites Umaru over to make chocolates and gets nervous when Taihei, whom she has a crush on, joins in.

Vegetable or canola oil, for greasing

1 pound good-quality chocolate (dark, milk, or white)

Toppings of your choice, such as dried fruits, nuts, or crumbled rice crackers, perferably Kakitane (optional)

1 Line a large baking sheet with parchment paper, and lay out several small to medium cookie cutters. Dip a folded paper towel lightly into a small bowl of oil and wipe around the inside of each cookie cutter. Place the cookie cutters on the baking sheet in a way that can fit all of them.

2 Chop the chocolate finely, then place two-thirds of it into a medium, heatproof bowl.

3 Pour 2 inches of water into a medium pot over medium heat and bring to a boil. Once the water is boiling, turn off the heat and remove the pot from the stove. Place the bowl of chopped chocolate on top of the steaming pot. Heat the chocolate until it reaches 115°F for dark chocolate or 110°F for milk and white chocolate, using a candy or digital thermometer.

4 Remove the bowl of chocolate from the pot and stir in the remaining third of chocolate. Continue stirring until the temperature of the chocolate is between 88°F and 90°F for dark chocolate, 84°F and 86°F for milk chocolate, or 82°F and 84°F for white chocolate.

5 Spoon a small amount of the melted chocolate onto a piece of parchment paper and smear it. After a few minutes, if the chocolate has become hardened and shiny, it's ready to use. If it does not turn out this way, check the temperature of the melted chocolate in the bowl and let it cool a bit more, or gently heat it above the pan of hot water to get to the right temperature.

6 Spoon melted chocolate into each prepared cookie cutter on the baking sheet, filling the cutters halfway. You can leave them plain, or you can sprinkle toppings on the chocolate before it solidifies. You can also put the toppings in the cookie cutter first, then pour the chocolate on top. Let the chocolates sit undisturbed for at least 5 minutes to harden. Umaru makes a unique chocolate combination with Kakitane rice snacks.

7 If you're not using all of the melted chocolate at this time, you can pour it into a parchment paper–lined dish to harden and re-temper it when you need it. Store the valentine chocolates and any hardened unused chocolate in an airtight container in an odorless, cool, dry, and dark place for up to 3 months.

NOTES Another type of chocolate mentioned in the Valentine's Day episode of *Himouto! Umaru-chan* is nama chocolate. This is very easy to make because it doesn't require tempering and uses only two ingredients: chocolate and heavy cream. Line the bottom and sides of a loaf pan or 7-inch square pan with parchment paper. Finely chop 7 ounces of dark chocolate (60 percent cacao or higher) and place in a heatproof bowl. Pour ½ cup of heavy cream into a small pot over medium heat. Stir the cream constantly to keep the bottom from burning and to prevent a "skin" from forming on the top, until it reaches 170°F on a candy or digital thermometer. Pour the hot cream evenly over the chopped chocolate and let sit for 30 seconds before stirring with a silicone spatula. Stir until smooth. If there are unmelted bits, heat the bowl of chocolate in the microwave for 15 seconds, then stir again. Pour the chocolate mixture into the prepared pan and spread it out evenly. Lay a piece of plastic wrap directly on top of the chocolate and place the pan in the refrigerator to chill overnight. Remove the plastic wrap and invert the chocolate onto a cutting board, peeling off the parchment paper as well. Using a long non-serrated knife, cut the chocolate into 1-inch squares. Dust the top with cocoa powder sifted through fine mesh. Store in an airtight container in the refrigerator for up to a week.

Another Valentine's Day treat seen in anime such as *Kimi ni Todoke: From Me to You* and *The Disappearance of Nagato Yuki-chan* is chocolate cups. To make these, you'll need mini metallic candy cups (they look like little cupcake or muffin wrappers). If you have a mini muffin tin, place the candy cups in the muffin cups. If you don't have one, the candy cups should keep their shape relatively fine, but they might spread out a little bit. Pour melted tempered chocolate into the cups to within ⅛ inch of the top. If you'd like to add toppings, add them before the chocolate sets. If you'd like to add an ingredient inside, pour ¼ inch of chocolate into each cup, then place the ingredient in. Pour chocolate over the top to cover it.

You could also make chocolate-covered potato chips as seen in *Aikatsu!* or chocolate-dipped cherries like in *Chocolate no Maho*.

CULTURE FACTS Valentine's Day was introduced to Japan in the 1930s, but didn't gain traction until after the 1950s, when confectionery company Morozoff promoted it with chocolate hearts. The holiday gained popularity in the 1970s and became a day for ladies to give chocolates (or cookies; see page 126) to gents. The different variations are called tomo-choco for friends, giri-choco for acquaintances and coworkers, and honmei-choco for those special someones.

A month later, on March 14 (known as White Day in Japan, with white symbolizing purity), men reciprocate the gift with sugar cookies, marshmallows, more chocolates, or nonedible things such as jewelry or white ribbons, like in the anime *Fruits Basket*. This holiday actually started in 1977 as Marshmallow Day, thought up by the confectionery company Ishimura Manseido K.K. In 1978 all candy companies were invited to participate, and it became known as White Day.

THIS FOOD ALSO APPEARS IN . . .

- *The Disappearance of Nagato Yuki-chan*
- *Kimi ni Todoke: From Me to You*
- *Tanaka-kun Is Always Listless*
- *Monthly Girls' Nozaki-Kun*
- *Place to Place*
- *Orange*
- *Nisekoi*
- *My Love Story!!*
- *Toradora!*
- *Aqua Age*

GO! PRINCESS PRECURE

ANMITSU

Agar Jelly with Sweet Syrup and Fruit

SERVES 2 Cheerful Haruka Haruno refuses to give up on her dream of becoming a princess despite being bullied for it when she's little. While attending Noble Academy, Haruka meets friends, fairies, and villains—and learns of a witchy plot to lock away the world's dreams! With newfound powers and allies, Haruka fights a plethora of despair-spreading baddies, all while studying for school and learning princessly attributes. Summer vacation gives Haruka and her friends time to unwind, and to help serve anmitsu at her family's restaurant.

1/2 cup plus 2 tablespoons granulated sugar
1/2 cup dark brown or muscovado sugar
2 teaspoons agar agar powder
2 scoops of Matcha Ice Cream (page 132)
1/2 cup Anko Sweet Red Bean Paste (page 99)
4 to 6 Dango (page 118)
Fresh fruit, such as cherries, kiwi, bananas, mandarin oranges, or apple slices

1 In a medium pot over medium heat, combine 1/2 cup water, 1/2 cup granulated sugar, and the brown sugar. Bring the mixture to a low boil, stirring occasionally, then reduce the heat to low. Simmer for 20 minutes until all of the sugar has dissolved and the mixture has thickened slightly. Remove the pot from the stove and let the mixture cool to room temperature. Pour into a small pitcher and set aside until needed. This syrup is called kuromitsu.

2 In a medium pot over medium-high heat, combine 2 cups of water with the agar agar powder. Bring to a boil to dissolve the powder, then reduce the heat to medium and stir in 2 tablespoons granulated sugar. Cook until the sugar is dissolved, then remove the pot from the heat to cool for 5 minutes. Pour the mixture into an 8 x 8-inch baking dish. Cover with plastic wrap and place in the refrigerator for at least 30 minutes to chill and solidify.

3 Once the agar jelly has solidified, remove it from the refrigerator and run a thin knife blade around the inside of the dish. Invert the agar jelly onto a cutting board and slice it into 1/2-inch cubes. Divide the cubes equally between 2 dessert bowls. Place a scoop of matcha ice cream on top of each, along with 1/4 cup of anko, 2 to 3 dango, and several fruit slices of your choice. Serve the anmitsu with the kuromitsu syrup on the side.

FOOD FACTS You can be creative with what toppings you'd like to add to anmitsu. The dango can be plain or colorful like Hinami Dango (page 118), or made with an indentation instead of a round shape so they cook faster. Kuromame, or sweet boiled black beans, are a common addition, and sometimes sweetened chestnuts are added. Kinako powder, which is made from roasted soybeans, is sometimes served on the side. You can leave off the ice cream or change up the flavor. You can even add matcha powder while preparing the agar jelly so you end up with pretty green cubes, as seen in *Okko's Inn*, served with anko and dango. If you'd like to make matcha agar jelly, whisk 2 teaspoons culinary-grade matcha green tea powder with 1 tablespoon very hot water. Whisk into the pot of agar liquid once you've removed the pot from the stove to cool. Anmitsu really is a beautiful and versatile dish!

Kuromitsu means "black honey" in Japanese and is used on many different sweet treats, or wagashi. It's lovely on Matcha Ice Cream (page 132), Parfaits (page 128), Mochi coated with kinako soybean powder and sugar (page 116), Dango (page 118), Kakigori (page 104), and more.

ANIME FACTS Did you know that there is both a 1949 manga and a 1986 anime named *Anmitsu Hime*? *Hime* means "princess" in Japanese, and this precocious princess lives in the Amakura Kingdom, which means "sweet and spicy," just like her personality. She even has a tutor named Castella from the Pudding Kingdom, castella being a popular cake in Japan originally introduced by Portuguese merchants. Other food characters include Manju, Ohagi, and Senbei, all types of Japanese sweets and treats.

THIS FOOD ALSO APPEARS IN . . .

- *Sweet Blue Flowers*
- *Is the Order a Rabbit?*
- *Kantai Collection*
- *Yotsuiro Biyori*
- *Recovery of an MMO Junkie*
- *Fuuka*
- *Go! Princess PreCure*
- *Urara Meirocho*
- *March Comes in Like a Lion*
- *Okko's Inn*

THE DISASTROUS LIFE OF SAIKI K.

COFFEE JELLY

SERVES 2 TO 4 Born with extreme psychic abilities, teenager Kusuo Saiki tries to shroud his life in mediocrity so as not to draw attention to himself. Over the course of his high school days, however, he gets caught up in the troubles and antics of those around him. It's such a bother, when all he wants is peace and quiet and the occasional delicious coffee jelly . . .

- **½ cup coarse-ground coffee beans**
- **2 cups cold water**
- **2 teaspoons agar agar powder or gelatin powder**
- **3 tablespoons granulated sugar**

FOR THE WHIPPED CREAM

- **1 cup heavy cream, chilled**
- **½ teaspoon vanilla extract (optional)**
- **2 tablespoons powdered sugar**
- **Pinch of cream of tartar (optional)**

1 Pour the coffee grounds into a large jar and cover with the cold water. Stir the mixture gently so that the grounds don't come up on the sides of the jar. Close the jar and place in the refrigerator to chill overnight. The next day, strain the cold-brew coffee into a medium pot through a cheesecloth, nut milk cloth, or a coffee filter set in a fine-mesh strainer. You want to strain out all of the coffee bean particles.

2 Add the agar agar or gelatin powder and sugar to the pot with the coffee and turn the heat to medium. Bring the mixture to a boil, whisking a few times at the beginning. Once boiling, remove from the heat and let cool for 5 minutes. Divide the mixture between 2 to 4 cups, depending on your preference, and let them sit on the counter until the mixture reaches room temperature. Place in the refrigerator and chill overnight, or until fully solidified.

3 Make the whipped cream: Pour the heavy cream and vanilla, if desired, into a chilled mixing bowl and sift in the powdered sugar and cream of tartar, if using. Mix on medium speed just until stiff peaks form. If you'd like to pipe whipped cream onto the coffee jelly, scoop the whipped cream into a piping bag with a snipped corner or a sturdy zip-top bag; piping tips optional.

4 Remove the containers of coffee jelly from the refrigerator. Gently run a knife around the inside edges of the cups to loosen the jelly, then invert the cups onto serving dishes. You may need to tap the overturned cups for the jelly to plop out. Add the whipped cream to the jelly by piping it or simply adding a dollop on top.

NOTES Cubed coffee jelly is also popular in Japan. Instead of pouring the coffee and agar mixture into individual cups, pour it into a flat baking dish and chill it. Once it's set, slice the jelly into cubes and place them in a cup. Pour milk, half-and-half, or flavored coffee creamer on top, or a combination of equal parts condensed milk and heavy cream, or whatever meets your tastes!

Instant coffee can be used in this recipe to save time, but cold brew coffee is so much nicer—smoother and less acidic. If you don't have the time or the beans, however, simply skip the overnight coffee brewing and add 1½ tablespoons of instant coffee crystals to 2 cups of boiling water with the same amounts of agar agar powder and sugar, and continue the recipe as is.

CULTURE FACTS Despite being introduced by traders in the 1700s, coffee didn't fully take off in Japan until the 1950s, after World War II (although there were many coffee houses in the '30s and earlier, import bans were put in place during WWII). Because of Westernization and the allure of foreign tastes, the popularity of coffee grew in cafés around the country, with another spike in popularity once canned coffee hit the market in 1969.

In anime, coffee is often shown as a sophisticated drink and can be used as a symbol of a character's steps to maturity and adulthood, as in *Holmes of Kyoto*.

Coffee jelly, which has existed in England and America since the 1800s, was actually adapted to Japanese tastes using agar agar in the early 1900s but didn't enter the mainstream until later. Though still available in New England in the US, coffee jelly these days is most often considered a Japanese dessert because of its prevalence in cafés and konbini (convenience stores).

THIS FOOD ALSO APPEARS IN . . .

- *Ranma ½*
- *A Lull in the Sea*
- *Mr. Tonegawa: Middle Management Blues*
- *Kuroko's Basketball*

FLYING WITCH

POCKY

Chocolate-Covered Biscuit Sticks

MAKES 30 TO 35 Magic can be flashy and exciting, but is mostly built of subtleties, precision, and practice. Young witch Makoto moves in with her nonmagical relatives in a small suburb and continues to practice her magic, inspiring her little cousin Chinatsu. Makoto's older sister, Akane, who is more experienced in the magical arts, comes to visit and agrees to give Chinatsu a deeper look into the world of witches. The first demonstration is a small spell involving pocky, and results in uncontrollable tears and laughter.

- **⅓ cup all-purpose flour**
- **¼ cup non-glutinous rice flour**
- **1 tablespoon sugar**
- **¼ teaspoon baking powder**
- **¼ teaspoon salt**
- **1 tablespoon unsalted butter, diced**
- **1 tablespoon plus 2 teaspoons milk**
- **½ teaspoon vanilla extract**
- **35 bamboo chopsticks**
- **Tempered chocolate (see page 120)**

1 Sift together the flours, sugar, baking powder, and salt in a medium bowl. Using your fingers, work in the butter until the mixture becomes crumbly. Stir in the milk and vanilla and knead the mixture until a cohesive dough forms. Wrap the dough in plastic wrap and let it rest on the counter for 30 minutes.

2 Unwrap the dough and roll it into a 6-inch rectangle about 1/8 inch thick. Using a ruler to get equal measurements, cut the dough into ⅛-inch-wide strips that are 6 inches long. A pizza cutter or bench scraper works well for this. Keep the strips straight. Reroll the dough as necessary until it's all used up. Gently roll each strip evenly lengthwise to round out the edges slightly.

3 Line a large baking sheet with parchment paper and gather up the bamboo chopsticks. Lay a chopstick on the baking sheet, place a dough strip against it, then place another chopstick on the dough strip's other side. Repeat this alternating pattern so that each dough strip is held snuggly and straight by two chopsticks. Place the baking sheet in the refrigerator to chill for 10 minutes.

4 Preheat the oven to 300°F. Slide the baking sheet of dough sticks onto the middle rack of the oven and bake for 18 to 20 minutes, or until the biscuit edges are beginning to brown. Remove from the oven and let the biscuit sticks rest on the baking sheet for 5 minutes before removing the chopsticks and transferring the biscuits to a cooling rack.

5 Set up a large styrofoam block or cake pop holder on the counter to hold the Pocky after it's been dipped. If using styrofoam, use a chopstick to pre-poke holes 2 inches apart and ½ inch deep. You can also use the holes on the sides of a colander to hold the Pocky, though it can be trickier to balance them.

6 Once the biscuit sticks are cooled, prepare a batch of tempered chocolate.

7 Dip each biscuit stick into the chocolate, leaving a 1-inch space chocolate-free where you're holding the stick. Let any excess chocolate drip from the Pocky back into the bowl. Carefully place the coated Pocky upright in the premade holes in the styrofoam, or in the cake pop stand or colander.

8 Let the Pocky sit undisturbed for at least 5 minutes for the chocolate to solidify. If you'd like to add toppings such as chopped nuts or chopped dried fruit, do so right after dipping and before standing the sticks upright in the holder. To store the Pocky, keep them in an airtight container in a cool, dry, dark place. Store the excess tempered chocolate this way as well, after letting it harden on parchment paper. You can reuse the chocolate later.

FOOD FACTS Pocky, sold by Glico since 1966, is such a common and well-loved snack in Japan that it often makes its way into anime, sometimes in the forefront of a scene, but usually quietly in the background, like in the back seat of the car in *Spirited Away*.

The name Pocky, pronounced with a long *o* sound, comes from the Japanese word *pokkin*, which is an onomatopoeia for the sound a long stick makes when snapped. The derivative word *poki* is the sound the Pocky biscuit makes when you bite it (*poki* is a common sound effect in manga for "snap"). Often Pocky's name is changed in anime because of copyright reasons, so, for example, in *Flying Witch* (and *A Certain Scientific Railgun*), we get chocolate-covered biscuit sticks called "koppi" instead. Other names include "Rocky" (*Anohana*, *A Town Where You Live*), "Packy" (*Shirobako*, *Slow Start*), "Picky" (*Sweetness & Lightning*), "Pucky" (*Hidamari Sketch*), "Pony" (*Scum's Wish*), "Kocky" (*Tamako Market*), "Lucky" (*Tsukigakirei*), and many others.

CULTURE FACTS Have you heard of the Pocky game? You can see it in anime like *Kämpfer* and *Grand Blue Dreaming*, though the huge Pocky stick in the latter is not recommended. To play, two people take one end of a Pocky stick in their mouths and bite toward the center, and the object is to see who will pull away first. It's a bit like playing chicken. You'll sometimes see male idol groups playing the Pocky game for fan service. This Pocky-action is also called a Pocky kiss, kind of like the spaghetti scene in *Lady and the Tramp*.

November 11 is National Pocky Day, or *pokki no hi*, in Japan, because 11/11 looks like a handful of Pocky sticks. This unofficial holiday was instituted by Glico in 1999 in response to their Korean competitor Lotte's declaration of "Pepero Day" in 1997—Pepero being Lotte's imitation of Pocky. Glico's waiting two years to retaliate was calculated for maximum stick-number effect, because 1999 was the eleventh year of Heisei (the eleventh year on the throne of the emperor at the time), making the first Pocky Day fall on 11/11/11.

THIS FOOD ALSO APPEARS IN . . .

- *Grand Blue Dreaming*
- *Sket Dance*
- *Tari Tari*
- *Hyakko*
- *K-On!*
- *Saekano: How to Raise a Boring Girlfriend*
- *Humanity Has Declined*
- *One Week Friends*
- *Puella Magi Madoka Magica*
- *Kämpfer*
- *WataMote*
- *Ga-Rei-Zero*
- *Comic Girls*
- *Anohana: The Flower We Saw That Day*
- *Akame ga Kill!*
- *Rascal Does Not Dream of Bunny Girl Senpai*

SAILOR MOON

PARFAIT

Layered Dessert

SERVES 2 After rescuing a black cat with a strange marking on its forehead, clumsy crybaby Usagi Tsukino discovers that she's actually the guardian of love and justice, Sailor Moon! While Usagi battles baddies from the Dark Kingdom and encounters more Sailor allies, her best friend, Naru, falls in love with a Dark Kingdom general disguised as a human. Astrological plans, pining, manipulations, and ambushes ensue, along with a change of heart and dreams of sharing a chocolate parfait.

FOR THE MOUSSE

2 ounces semisweet baking chocolate, finely chopped

1 cup heavy cream

2 large egg whites, at room temperature

1 tablespoon sugar

FOR THE BROWNIES

1 ounce semisweet baking chocolate, finely chopped

¼ cup unsalted butter

¼ cup sugar

½ teaspoon vanilla extract

1 large egg, at room temperature

¼ cup all-purpose flour

Pinch of baking powder

Pinch of salt

FOR THE FUDGE SAUCE

3 ounces semisweet baking chocolate, finely chopped

½ cup evaporated milk, at room temperature

2 tablespoons sugar

2 tablespoons unsalted butter

Pinch of salt

FOR SERVING

Whipped Cream (page 124)

½ cup chocolate cookie crumbles or crispy chocolate cereal

1 banana, sliced

Other chocolate crunchy sweets, to add more texture (optional)

2 scoops chocolate or vanilla ice cream

4 Pocky (page 126)

2 to 4 cookies or wafers

Fresh mint leaves (optional)

1 First, make the mousse: Pour 2 inches of water into a medium pot over medium heat and bring to a boil. Place the chocolate in a medium, heatproof bowl. Once the water is boiling, turn off the heat and remove the pot from the stove. Place the bowl of chocolate on top of the steaming pot and let the chocolate melt, stirring often. Set aside until needed. In a mixing bowl, whisk the heavy cream until it increases in volume and holds soft peaks when the whisk is lifted. In another bowl, whisk the egg whites and sugar until they also have soft peaks. Gently fold the melted chocolate into the egg-white mixture until combined, then fold in the whipped cream. Cover the bowl and chill in the refrigerator for 1 hour.

2 Meanwhile, make the brownies: Preheat the oven to 350°F. Line the bottom of a 9 x 5-inch loaf pan with parchment paper. Pour 2 inches of water into a medium pot over medium heat and bring to a boil. Place the chocolate, butter, and sugar in a medium heatproof bowl. Once the water is boiling, turn off the heat and remove the pot from the stove. Place the bowl on top of the steaming pot and let the ingredients melt, stirring often. Once fully melted, place the bowl on the counter and stir in the vanilla extract. Quickly whisk in the egg until fully combined. Sift the flour, baking powder, and salt into the bowl and whisk until just combined. Pour the batter into the prepared pan and spread it out evenly. Bake for 15 to 20 minutes, or until a toothpick inserted into the center comes out clean. Let it cool in the pan, then run a knife around the edges to loosen it. Invert onto a cutting board and cut into ½-inch cubes. Transfer to an airtight container and leave on the counter until needed.

3 Next, make the fudge sauce: Melt the chocolate as in step 1. Once the chocolate is completely melted, add the evaporated milk, sugar, butter, and salt and stir until completely combined and smooth. Pour the sauce into a small pitcher or cup with a pour spout. You can use it warm or let it come to room temperature. Store leftover sauce in an airtight container in the refrigerator for up to a month. Re-melt it in the microwave in short intervals, stirring often.

4 To assemble the parfait, place several of the brownie cubes in the bottom of a tall parfait or sundae glass. Spoon a layer of mousse on top of the cubes. Sprinkle in a layer of cookie bits or cereal. Place several banana slices around the side of the glass above the crunchy layer, then pipe whipped cream into the center to the top of the banana slices. Place extra crunchy chocolate candy, if using, on top of the whipped cream and add a scoop of ice cream in the center. Pipe more whipped cream on and around the ice cream if you'd like, then drizzle on the fudge sauce. Decorate the parfait with more banana slices, the Pocky, cookies or wafers, and mint, if desired. Serve immediately with a long-handled spoon.

NOTE Because parfait is a multilayered dessert, it can be tedious (but so delicious!) to make the layer ingredients at home. Feel free to make what you'd like and then substitute premade ingredients for the rest, even changing up what's in each layer if you want. The idea behind a Japanese parfait is not only to look visually appealing but to have different textures as well, like the smooth mousse, the soft brownies, and the crunchy cereal or broken-up cookies in this recipe. You could substitute pudding, yogurt, cake pieces, granola, nuts, various fruits, Dango (page 118), Anko Sweet Red Bean Paste (page 99)—choose what you like, and get creative!

FOOD FACTS Choco-banana is a popular flavor in Japan, but it is by no means the only one! Strawberry parfait is also super popular and can be seen in *Akame ga Kill!*, *Gintama*, and *Gabriel Dropout*. Matcha parfait, as seen in *After the Rain* and *Yotsuiro Biyori*, is another popular choice. Parfait mixed with fresh fruit, like in *Inu x Boku SS*, *Canaan*, and *Bunny Drop*, are beautiful, delicious, and refreshing. Some parfait even have Purin (page 114) on top like in *K-On!*.

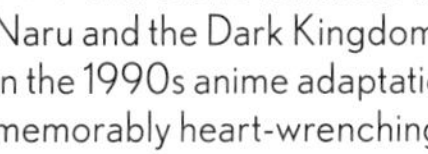

ANIME FACTS In the original *Sailor Moon* manga, there is no romance or talk of chocolate parfait between Naru and the Dark Kingdom general Nephrite. That was added in the 1990s anime adaptation, and leads to one of the most memorably heart-wrenching scenes in the show.

THIS FOOD ALSO APPEARS IN . . .

- *Gintama*
- *Vampire Princess Miyu*
- *Ranma ½*
- *Tokyo Ghoul: Root A*
- *After the Rain*
- *3D Kanojo: Real Girl*
- *Fuuka*
- *Rainy Cocoa*
- *Gabriel Dropout*
- *Someday's Dreamers*
- *Chocolate no Maho*
- *Zombieland Saga*
- *Love, Chunibyu & Other Delusions! Take on Me*
- *Urusei Yatsura*
- *Bodacious Space Pirates*
- *BLEND-S*
- *A Certain Scientific Railgun*
- *Vampire Knight*

MY TEEN ROMANTIC COMEDY SNAFU

CHECKERBOARD COOKIES

MAKES 2 DOZEN COOKIES Ostracized high schooler Hachiman Hikigaya doesn't believe in the happiness of youth and thinks that those who do are just fooling themselves. After being thrust into the Service Club to help those in need by a perceptive teacher who wants to reform his outlook, Hachiman meets and gradually befriends several students, all in varying stages of discovering their "true" selves. Cookies appear every so often—made to express feelings while maybe not tasting great, tasting very good but being kept aside out of worry, and being given as an offering in hopes that things will stay the same.

- **½ cup unsalted butter**
- **¼ teaspoon salt**
- **1 egg yolk, at room temperature**
- **1 teaspoon vanilla extract**
- **1 cup all-purpose flour**
- **½ cup powdered sugar**
- **1 tablespoon dark chocolate cocoa powder**

1 In a large mixing bowl, beat the butter and salt until creamy, 1 to 2 minutes. Add the egg yolk and vanilla extract and continue to beat to combine well. Sift in the flour and powdered sugar and beat on medium-low until a cohesive dough forms, 1 to 2 minutes. Shape the dough into a ball, flatten it into a thick disk, and divide equally in half. Place half of the dough back in the mixing bowl and sift in the cocoa powder. Mix on medium-low until the dough is a uniform chocolate color.

2 Shape the plain dough into a thick log and lay it on a large sheet of plastic wrap. Wrap the dough and shape it into a rectangle with square ends, 3½ inches long by 1½ inches wide; dropping the dough onto a flat surface or using a flat spatula can help shape the sides. Repeat with the chocolate dough, place both dough blocks on a plate, and put the plate into the refrigerator to chill for 1 hour.

3 Remove the dough from the refrigerator. Unwrap it and use a large sharp knife to cut both blocks in half lengthwise. Lay the chocolate halves on the plain halves, putting the cut sides together and lining them up on all sides. Cut both blocks lengthwise again. Place the cut halves together as before, this time making sure the chocolate and plain are alternating and that the corners line up to create a checkerboard pattern on the ends. Wrap the blocks tightly in plastic and reshape as needed. Place back in the refrigerator for at least 2 hours, or overnight.

4 Line a large baking sheet with parchment paper. Remove the cookie dough from the refrigerator and unwrap. Using a long, sharp knife, slice the sides of the blocks very thinly to flatten and even them out into concise rectangles. Next, slice the blocks into ¼-inch-thick squares, rotating the blocks after each cut to keep them uniform. Lay the cookie slices on the baking sheet at least 1 inch apart. Place the baking sheet in the refrigerator while you preheat your oven to 350°F.

5 Slide the baking sheet onto the middle oven rack and bake for 10 to 12 minutes, or until the bottoms are just beginning to turn golden. Remove from the oven and let the cookies sit on the baking sheet for a minute before transferring them to a cooling rack.

FOOD FACTS These cookies are sometimes called icebox cookies, checkerboard icebox cookies, or chess cookies. They're European in origin, often found in Germany, Sweden, and France, and have become very popular in Japan.

THIS FOOD ALSO APPEARS IN . . .

- *Humanity Has Declined*
- *Lucky Star*
- *Baka and Test: Summon the Beasts*
- *Saint Seiya*
- *Hina Logic—from Luck & Logic*
- *Himouto! Umaru-chan*
- *THE IDOLM@STER*
- *Please Tell Me! Galko-chan*
- *Wataten!: An Angel Flew Down to Me*
- *Date a Live*
- *Jewelpet Sunshine*
- *Go! Princess PreCure*
- *Ginga e Kickoff!!*
- *Toradora!*
- *Sound! Euphonium*
- *Hyakko*
- *Boarding School Juliet*
- *The Quintessential Quintuplets*
- *One Week Friends*
- *K-On!*
- *Penguindrum*

KIKI'S DELIVERY SERVICE

HOTTOKEKI

Thick Pancakes

SERVES 2 Thirteen-year-old witch Kiki sets out with her cat, Jiji, into the wide world to find the town that she will settle in to begin her magic-based profession. She chooses a beautiful seaside town that hasn't had a witch in decades, and moves into a room above a bakery. While setting up her business and going through the pains of growing up, Kiki pretty much lives off pancakes.

1 cup cake flour
1 teaspoon baking powder
Pinch of salt
1 egg, at room temperature
2 tablespoons sugar
½ cup buttermilk, at room temperature
1 tablespoon melted butter
1 teaspoon vanilla extract
1 teaspoon vegetable or canola oil

1 Sift the flour, baking powder, and salt into a medium bowl. In a separate medium bowl, whisk the egg and sugar vigorously until pale, then whisk in the milk, butter, and vanilla. Pour the liquid gradually into the bowl of dry ingredients, whisking from the center to the edges to combine.

2 Heat a skillet or large pan over medium-low heat and add the oil, spreading it around the bottom of the pan using a paper towel. Using a measuring cup, scoop out ⅓ cup of batter and hold it 3 inches above the center of the pan, then pour it out to create a circle. Cover the pan with a lid and cook for 1½ minutes, until small bubbles form and the top is still wet. Remove the lid and carefully flip the pancake. Cover again and cook for 2½ minutes, until the bottom is golden brown. Transfer to a plate and cover with a large sheet of plastic wrap to keep in the moisture and some of the heat. Repeat the cooking process with the rest of the batter.

NOTE If you don't have buttermilk, simply pour 1½ teaspoons of lemon juice or white vinegar into a liquid measuring cup and add in milk up to the ½ cup line. Stir and let it sit for 5 minutes, and then it's ready to use!

FOOD FACTS Hotcakes and pancakes are used interchangeably. In Japan, pancakes are often associated with savory pairings that can be part of a meal, and hotcakes as a sweeter dish for a teatime snack. We see Kiki eating her hotcakes with sausage and tomatoes in the film, though, which might be influenced by the non-Japanese setting, but most likely by Kiki's need for frugality.

Soufflé pancakes are also popular in Japan and can be seen in *Food Wars!* and *Your Name*. These are made by separating the egg yolks and whites and whipping the whites into a meringue before folding it into the rest of the batter. Often a tall, round mold is used for the batter in the pan, but if the batter can hold its shape, it's piped in the pan instead.

ANIME FACTS In *Kiki's Delivery Service*, Kiki uses a mix called Jiburi no Hottokeki, which means "Jiburi's Hotcakes," Jiburi being phonetic for Ghibli, the animation studio that made the film.

Kiki is based on the book series *Maho no Takkyuubin*, or "Witch's Delivery Service," by Eiko Kadono.

Kadono came up with Gutiokipanja for the name of the bakery as a play on "gu, choki, pan," or "rock, scissors, paper." The name also contains *gut*, which is German for "good," and *pan*, which is Japanese (via Portuguese and Latin) for "bread." *Panya* is also the Japanese word for "bakery."

Along with hotcakes, Okayu Porridge (page 30) and many other baked goods including a special chocolate cake appear in *Kiki*. Herring and pumpkin pie is a memorable dish from the film that also appears as an easter egg in *Silver Spoon*. This isn't a Japanese food but is inspired by herring dishes in Sweden, where much of the film is set. And perhaps, as a stretch, inspiration might have come from the title of an old book for German immigrants to the United States titled *Herring and Pumpkin Pie*. Another Swedish-inspired herring pie, found in *Little Witch Academia*, is called *hapansilakka*, which means "Baltic herring," and is shaped like a Karelian rye crust pastry.

THIS FOOD ALSO APPEARS IN . . .

- *Sailor Moon*
- *Polar Bear Café*
- *Flying Witch*
- *Last Exile -Fam, the Silver Wing-*
- *A-Channel*
- *Space Dandy*
- *Eureka 7: AO*
- *The Ones Within*
- *Hi Score Girl*
- *Your Name*
- *Charlotte*
- *Alice & Zoroku*
- *Cardcaptor Sakura*
- *Himouto! Umaru-chan R*
- *Chibi Devi!*
- *Is the Order a Rabbit?*
- *Upotte!!*
- *Show By Rock!!*
- *Little Busters! Refrain*
- *ACCA*
- *Alice or Alice*
- *Parasyte -the maxim-*

DEATH NOTE

MATCHA ICE CREAM

Ice Cream Made with Powdered Green Tea

SERVES 6 Finding a strange notebook purposefully dropped by a bored god of death, Light Yagami takes it upon himself to anonymously execute those he deems in need of being purged from society by writing their names and causes of death in the fatal book. The aloof genius L is brought in to help the police track down the mysterious killer, and more often than not, L can be found perched in his chair, consuming sweet treats. Sometimes he'll even share his ice cream.

3 large egg yolks
1/2 cup sugar
Pinch of salt
2 tablespoons culinary-quality matcha green tea powder
3/4 cup whole milk
1/2 teaspoon vanilla extract
1 cup heavy cream

1 If you have an ice cream maker, make sure to freeze the bowl before proceeding. Whisk the egg yolks, sugar, and salt in a medium bowl until very pale and creamy. Sift in the matcha and whisk until the green is evenly distributed. Adding more matcha will give a stronger bitter flavor, so add according to your taste.

2 In a medium pot, heat the milk and vanilla over medium-low heat, just until the milk is heated through and beginning to steam, with little bubbles forming around the sides. Remove the pot from the heat and whisk 1 tablespoon of the milk into the matcha egg yolk mixture until it's fully incorporated. Gradually add more warm milk to the yolk mixture, whisking well after each addition, until thoroughly combined.

3 Strain the mixture through a fine-mesh strainer into the medium pot. Cook over medium-low heat, stirring constantly, until the temperature reaches 170°F on a digital or candy thermometer and the mixture has thickened slightly, forming a custard. Remove from the heat.

4 Whisk the heavy cream into the matcha custard until smooth and combined. Strain the mixture through a fine-mesh strainer into an airtight, freezer-safe container. Cut a piece of parchment paper to lay directly on top of the mixture, then close the container and place it in the refrigerator overnight.

5 The next day, pour the ice cream mixture into the frozen bowl of your ice cream maker and follow your maker's instructions to churn it. Once the machine is finished, scoop the ice cream back into the container, cut a piece of parchment paper to lay directly on top of the ice cream, and freeze it overnight. Alternatively, if you don't have an ice cream maker, pour the refrigerated mixture into a shallow container or baking dish and place in the freezer for 30 minutes. Take out of the freezer and use a handheld mixer to beat the ice cream and break up any ice bits. Place back in the freezer for 30 minutes, then beat again. Repeat this for 2 to 3 hours until the ice cream is solid. Scoop the ice cream into an airtight freezer container, with parchment directly on top of the ice cream, and keep it in the freezer until you're ready to serve.

FOOD FACTS The matcha ice cream in *Death Note* is served in cones (three scoops for L and police chief Yagami, two for everybody else) but you can simply serve it in a bowl. It's also a wonderful addition to Parfaits (page 128), Crepes (page 103), Anmitsu (page 123), Mochi (page 116), and Kakigori (page 104), as seen in anime like *After the Rain*, *Yotsuiro Biyori*, and *Is the Order a Rabbit?*.

ANIME FACTS Aside from matcha ice cream, there are many other foods in *Death Note*, such as apples, strawberry cake, candies, chips with little TVs in the bag, prosciutto on melon, more apples, and more sweets. So many sweets. Because L's food consumption is so prevalent, there has been speculation about why his character eats so many sweets. Considering that he's a genius and that the brain, out of all the other organs in the body, demands the most energy—energy that's converted from glucose, which in turn comes from sugars and starches—his eating habits make sense (he does say that using his brain keeps him thin), though too much glucose to the brain can be detrimental. L's eating habits, and even the way he eats and holds objects in general, are also simply ways to add to the strangeness of the character.

Matcha ice cream isn't the only green ice cream in anime: others include mint, melon, and even wasabi in *B-Project* and kombu kelp in *Aikatsu Stars!*.

THIS FOOD ALSO APPEARS IN . . .

- *My Love Story!!*
- *ACCA*
- *Yotsuiro Biyori*
- *Tari Tari*
- *Is the Order a Rabbit?*
- *After the Rain*

MATCHA ROLL CAKE

Sponge Cake Roll with Cream Inside

SERVES 6 TO 8 With a palate for flavor and a stomach for sweets, Ichigo Amano ends up attending the prestigious St. Marie's Academy, the same school her famous pâtissiere grandmother attended. Ichigo has a ton to learn, but with a strong desire for sweets and smiles, and a helpful little fairy, her dreams are within reach. When she learns that the little brother of her classmate Andou-kun, who comes from a Japanese confectionery dynasty, hates cake, she helps make a delicious roll cake using bitter matcha, subtle cream, and homemade sweet bean paste—a perfect fusion to convey the brothers' feelings.

FOR THE MATCHA SPONGE CAKE

1/3 cup plus 1 tablespoon cake flour

2 tablespoons culinary-grade matcha powder

Pinch of salt

4 large egg whites, at room temperature

1/4 cup sugar

2 large egg yolks, at room temperature

1/4 cup vegetable or canola oil

1/2 teaspoon vanilla extract

FOR THE FILLING

2 tablespoons powdered sugar, plus more for dusting

2 teaspoons culinary-grade matcha powder, plus more for dusting

1 cup heavy cream

1/3 cup Anko Sweet Red Bean Paste, tsubuan version (page 98)

1 Place a medium mixing bowl in the freezer to chill. Preheat your oven to 350°F. Line a 9 x 13-inch baking dish with parchment paper, cutting the corners of the paper to fit nicely up the sides of the dish (for lifting the cake out later).

2 Sift the cake flour, matcha powder, and salt into a medium bowl. Sift into another bowl, then sift back into the first bowl.

3 In a large mixing bowl, use a hand mixer to whisk the egg whites until they hold soft peaks.

4 Add half of the sugar and whisk to combine, then add the rest of the sugar and whisk until stiff peaks form.

5 Use a whisk to fold in 1 egg yolk until combined, then add the other yolk and combine.

6 Sift a third of the flour and matcha mixture into the egg mixture, and use the whisk to gently fold it in. Add another third of the flour mixture and fold it in with the whisk, then add the rest of the flour and repeat.

7 Use a silicone spatula to gently fold in the oil and vanilla. Pour the batter evenly into the prepared baking dish and spread it out to fill the corners. Tap the dish on the counter a few times to release any air bubbles.

8 Place the dish on a large baking sheet and slide it into the oven. Bake for 12 minutes, or until the center of the cake is springy to the touch.

9 Remove the cake from the oven and lift it out of the baking dish using the edges of the parchment paper. Lay it on a cooling rack and peel the paper away from the sides. Lay a large, damp kitchen towel over the cake to prevent it from drying out.

10 Once the cake has cooled completely, make the filling: Sift the powdered sugar and matcha together into a small bowl and whisk to combine well. Remove the chilled mixing bowl from the freezer and pour in the heavy cream. Add the vanilla extract and sift in the powdered sugar mixture. Whisk with a hand mixer or stand mixer on high speed until the green color is evenly distributed, the cream increases in volume, and it holds medium-soft peaks when the whisk is lifted. Do not overmix.

11 Using the towel from on top of the cake, carefully flip the cake over. Peel away the parchment paper that was used during cooking; this should peel away the thin browned layer at the bottom of the cake as well. If there are any brown patches left, gently scrape them away with a knife. Lay a large sheet of clean parchment paper over the cake and flip it again so that the cake is sitting on the parchment paper. Remove the towel.

12 Use a long serrated knife to cut a declining angle from the edge of one of the short sides of the cake, so it looks like a little ramp. On the opposite end of the cake, make 3 shallow cuts widthwise, 1 inch apart. Position this end of the cake closest to you.

13 Spread the matcha whipped cream in an even layer over the cake, stopping just before you get to the ramp. Scoop the tsubuan anko in a thin line across the width of the cake, 3 inches up from the end closest to you.

14 Lift the edge closest to you and roll it up and over the anko, compacting it so there is no empty space, but making sure that you stay on top of the cream and don't press the cake down into it. Using the parchment paper can help to roll the cake. Continue to roll the cake tightly up toward the opposite end with the angled edge. Once you get to that edge, use the parchment paper to gently press the roll backwards to compact it. Keep the cake seam side down at this point to seal it closed.

15 Wrap the cake roll in the parchment, then in plastic wrap, and chill in the refrigerator (seam side down) for 1 to 2 hours. Before serving, you can sift powdered sugar or matcha powder on top if you'd like. To serve, use a serrated knife to slice the roll into pieces of your desired width. Wrap the leftover cake in plastic wrap and keep in the refrigerator for up to 2 days.

FOOD FACTS Aside from *Yumeiro Patissiere*, this matcha roll cake can be found in *Princess Jellyfish* as well, but instead of one thin line of anko, it's dispersed across the whole of the cream. Other versions of matcha roll cakes use anko whipped cream instead of matcha, or simply plain cream. Roll cake and Swiss roll cake are interchangeable terms in Japan. Strawberry, vanilla, chocolate, and many other flavors, sometimes with various fresh fruits rolled up inside, are also common and can be seen on tea-time tables and shop counters in many anime. In *Yumeiro Patissiere*, along with matcha, we get a chocolate and strawberry roll cake, as well as a chocolate and vanilla "angel and devil" fruit roll cake.

THIS FOOD ALSO APPEARS IN . . .

- *Magic Knight Rayearth*
- *Rin-ne*
- *ACCA*
- *Seiren*
- *Dropkick on My Devil!*
- *Panty & Stocking with Garterbelt*
- *Aikatsu!*
- *Sengoku Collection*
- *Is the Order a Rabbit?*
- *Polar Bear Café*
- *Hakuoki: Dawn of the Shinsengumi*
- *Nichijou—My Ordinary Life*
- *Love, Election and Chocolate*
- *Phi Brain*
- *Inu x Boku SS*
- *Cardcaptor Sakura: Clear Card*

ICHIGO NO SHOTOKEKI

Sponge Cake with Strawberries and Cream

MAKES 1 8-INCH CAKE Erza orders strawberry "Fantasia" cake from Magnolia Town's cake shop to welcome the Fairy Tail guild's newest member, Wendy—and orders another forty-nine just for herself! Their strawberry cake is her favorite, after all . . .

FOR THE SPONGE CAKE

6 large eggs, at room temperature

2/3 cup plus 1/4 cup granulated sugar

1/3 cup milk, at room temperature

3 tablespoons unsalted butter

1 1/3 cups cake flour, twice-sifted, plus more for dusting

41 fresh small strawberries of similar size

FOR THE WHIPPED CREAM

3 cups heavy cream

1 teaspoon vanilla extract

1/3 cup powdered sugar, sifted

1/4 teaspoon cream of tartar (optional)

1 Place a large mixing bowl in the freezer to chill until needed to make the whipped cream. Preheat the oven to 350°F and spray an 8-inch round cake pan with nonstick spray. Cut a circle of parchment paper to fit the bottom of the pan. Lightly flour the inside edges of the pan.

2 Pour 2 inches of water into a large pot and bring to a low simmer over medium-low heat.

3 Place the eggs and 2/3 cup sugar in a large, heatproof bowl and place the bowl over the pot of simmering water. Whisk the eggs and sugar, making sure the eggs don't solidify, and check the temperature often with a digital thermometer, removing the bowl from the heat when the mixture reaches 100°F.

4 Transfer the egg mixture to the bowl of a stand mixer and beat it with the whisk attachment on medium-high speed until fluffy and pale. Lift the whisk; if the mixture falls in a ribbon and stays for a few seconds before disappearing, you're good to go.

5 Combine the milk and butter in a small pot over medium heat. Stir and bring the temperature to 155°F. Remove from the heat and set aside.

6 Sift the cake flour into the fluffy egg and sugar mixture and quickly but gently fold it in with a spatula until fully combined, rotating the bowl often and being careful not to overmix.

7 Use your spatula as a scoop and scoop 2 spatulas-full of this batter into the milk and butter mixture. Stir well, then carefully pour the mixture over the flat side of the spatula into the bowl of batter. Fold the milk and butter mixture into the batter until fully incorporated and the batter falls like a ribbon when the spatula is lifted.

8 Pour the batter into the center of the prepared pan so that it spreads evenly. Smooth the top with an offset spatula or bench scraper if needed. Tap the pan on the counter a few times to release any air bubbles.

9 Bake for 20 minutes, or until the top is golden brown and springs back when lightly touched.

10 Remove the pan from the oven and drop it onto the counter from 8 inches high to shock the cake and prevent shrinkage. Run a thin knife around the edge of the pan and invert the cake onto a large plate. Gently peel the parchment paper off, then invert the cake again onto a cooling rack. Lay a damp paper towel over the cake to protect it from drying out. Let the cake cool to room temperature.

11 While the cake is baking, make simple syrup: Combine 1/4 cup sugar with 3 tablespoons water in a small bowl. Heat in the microwave for 1 1/2 to 2 minutes, or until the sugar is dissolved. Set aside to cool.

12 While the cake is cooling, make the whipped cream: Remove the chilled mixing bowl from the freezer and pour in the heavy cream and vanilla extract. Sift in the powdered sugar and cream of tartar, if using. Beat the mixture on high speed until light and fluffy and its peaks are of medium softness. Do not overmix.

13 Pat the strawberries with a damp paper towel to remove any dirt, then pat them dry. Remove the stems and leaves. Pick 11 of the prettiest strawberries of matching size to go on the top of the cake. Pick out 15 pretty strawberries to go around the sides of the cake. The remaining 15 strawberries will go inside.

14 Once the cake is cool, use a long serrated knife to carefully cut the cake in half horizontally through the center so that you end up with two equal cake rounds. Brush the cut sides of the cakes with the simple syrup.

15 Lay the bottom half of the cake, cut side up, on a cake plate or circle. Spread on a layer of whipped cream, ½ inch thick.

16 Place the 15 strawberries set aside for the sides of the cake around the very edge of this cake layer, gently pressing them into the whipped cream and spacing them equally apart, pointed ends up. Place 10 of the strawberries set aside for the inside of the cake in an even ring ½ inch away from the outer strawberries. Place the last 5 of the inside strawberries in an even ring ½ inch away from the ring of 10.

17 Spoon or pipe on more whipped cream to fill in the gaps between the strawberries and to bring the level of filling to the tops of the strawberries. Use an offset spatula to even the top of the filling.

18 Carefully lay the top layer of cake, cut side down, onto the filling layer. Brush the top of the cake with more of the simple syrup, then spread on a ¼-inch layer of whipped cream. Use an offset spatula to smooth out the edges of the cake, minding the strawberries peeking out around the middle.

19 Whip the remainder of the whipped cream until it holds stiff peaks. Scoop the cream into a piping bag with a medium star tip attached. Pipe a scalloped border around the top of the cake. Pipe 11 rosettes in a ring just inside the scalloped border with equal spacing between them. Gently press the 11 prettiest strawberries onto these rosettes, pointed ends up. Pipe whipped cream stars between the strawberries.

20 Cover the cake with a cake dome or very large bowl (not plastic wrap) and chill in the refrigerator for at least 1 hour. To serve, cut the cake with a long, sharp knife between the strawberries on top, wiping the knife clean after each cut.

NOTE This recipe uses the cake in the anime as a guide, but often shotokeki contain sliced strawberries in the center (halves or a bit thinner) instead of whole, while the whole strawberries are reserved for decorating the top.

If you'd like to make the chocolate Fairy Tail guild logo on top of the cake as seen in the show, draw the outline of the logo about 3 inches across in black Sharpie on a plain sheet of white paper. Flip the paper over and trace the design to create a mirror image of it. Use a small overturned bowl to draw a circle around the backwards logo. Melt ¼ cup of milk or dark chocolate and pour it into a candy decorating bag. Snip a small hole at the end of the bag. Lay the drawing under a sheet of parchment paper and trace and fill in the logo with the chocolate. Use a toothpick to create the fine details and points. Once the chocolate has hardened, melt ⅓ cup of white chocolate and pour it into another candy decorating bag, cutting a medium hole from the tip. Pipe the white chocolate over and around the logo to fill in the circle. Let the white chocolate harden completely, then carefully invert the chocolate design onto a plate and gently peel away the parchment paper, revealing the logo. Use a flat spatula to carefully transfer the chocolate logo to the top of the cake. Do this just before serving, while the cake is chilling in the refrigerator.

FOOD FACTS Strawberry shortcake, popular in Japan since the mid-1900s, was inspired by the American version, but instead of sandwiching strawberries and cream between the two halves of a biscuit or scone, the Japanese version uses fluffy sponge cake. This cake is often served on special occasions, like birthdays and Christmas, and can be seen in many anime for various celebratory reasons. Or you might find a character having a slice simply as a nice "treat yo self" snack.

THIS FOOD ALSO APPEARS IN . . .

- *JoJo's Bizarre Adventure: Golden Wind*
- *Nekopara*
- *Rozen Maiden*
- *Goldfish Warning!*
- *Kimi ni Todoke: From Me to You*
- *Cardcaptor Sakura*
- *3D Kanojo: Real Girl*
- *Sola*
- *Charlotte*
- *Prison School*
- *Yumeiro Patissiere*
- *Ace Attorney*
- *Girlish Number*
- *Eromanga Sensei*
- *Kuma Miko: Girl Meets Bear*
- *Erased*
- *Aikatsu!*
- *Chobits*
- *Endride*

METRIC CHARTS

The recipes that appear in this cookbook use the standard US method for measuring liquid and dry or solid ingredients (teaspoons, tablespoons, and cups). The information on these pages is provided to help cooks outside the United States successfully use these recipes. All equivalents are approximate.

METRIC EQUIVALENTS FOR DIFFERENT TYPES OF INGREDIENTS

A standard cup measure of a dry or solid ingredient will vary in weight depending on the type of ingredient. A standard cup of liquid is the same volume for any type of liquid. Use the following chart when converting standard cup measures to grams (weight) or milliliters (volume).

STANDARD CUP	FINE POWDER *(ex. flour)*	GRAIN *(ex. rice)*	GRANULAR *(ex. sugar)*	LIQUID SOLIDS *(ex. butter)*	LIQUID *(ex. milk)*
1	140 g	150 g	190 g	200 g	240 ml
¾	105 g	113 g	143 g	150 g	180 ml
⅔	93 g	100 g	125 g	133 g	160 ml
½	70 g	75 g	95 g	100 g	120 ml
⅓	47 g	50 g	63 g	67 g	80 ml
¼	35 g	38 g	48 g	50 g	60 ml
⅛	18 g	19 g	24 g	25 g	30 ml

USEFUL EQUIVALENTS FOR DRY INGREDIENTS BY WEIGHT

(To convert ounces to grams, multiply the number of ounces by 30.)

OZ	LB	G
1 oz	1/16 lb	30 g
4 oz	¼ lb	120 g
8 oz	½ lb	240 g
12 oz	¾ lb	360 g
16 oz	1 lb	480 g

USEFUL EQUIVALENTS FOR LENGTH

(To convert inches to centimeters, multiply the number of inches by 2.5.)

IN	FT	YD	CM	M
1 in			2.5 cm	
6 in	½ ft		15 cm	
12 in	1 ft		30 cm	
36 in	3 ft	1 yd	90 cm	
40 in			100 cm	1 m

USEFUL EQUIVALENTS FOR LIQUID INGREDIENTS BY VOLUME

TSP	TBSP	CUPS	FL OZ	ML	L
¼ tsp				1 ml	
½ tsp				2 ml	
1 tsp				5 ml	
3 tsp	1 Tbsp		½ fl oz	15 ml	
	2 Tbsp	⅛ cup	1 fl oz	30 ml	
	4 Tbsp	¼ cup	2 fl oz	60 ml	
	5 ⅓ Tbsp	⅓ cup	3 fl oz	80 ml	
	8 Tbsp	½ cup	4 fl oz	120 ml	
	10 ⅔ Tbsp	⅔ cup	5 fl oz	160 ml	
	12 Tbsp	¾ cup	6 fl oz	180 ml	
	16 Tbsp	1 cup	8 fl oz	240 ml	
	1 pt	2 cups	16 fl oz	480 ml	
	1 qt	4 cups	32 fl oz	960 ml	
			33 fl oz	1000 ml	1 l

USEFUL EQUIVALENTS FOR COOKING/OVEN TEMPERATURES

	FAHRENHEIT	CELSIUS	GAS MARK
FREEZE WATER	32° F	0° C	
ROOM TEMPERATURE	68° F	20° C	
BOIL WATER	212° F	100° C	
	325° F	160° C	3
	350° F	180° C	4
	375° F	190° C	5
	400° F	200° C	6
	425° F	220° C	7
	450° F	230° C	8
BROIL			Grill

ACKNOWLEDGMENTS

Kate and Anja at Tiller approached me with the idea of doing an anime cookbook, and I was so flattered and scared and excited. Over the course of this book's creation I'm sure Anja wanted to pull her hair out on numerous occasions because of me, and I want to thank her for being incredible in the face of my shortcomings.

Thank you, Samantha. And thank you, Patrick and Matt, for the book's design. And to Nero for the wonderful, delicious-looking art!

Thanks to my daughter and husband for putting up with an almost perpetually messy kitchen and lots of leftovers from So. Much. Recipe. Testing. And for being supportive when I had the occasional breakdown.

Thanks to my mom and dad, who let me mess around in the kitchen when I was younger and who made cooking seem accessible.

And thank you to my Moon, who passed away during the tail end of the making of this book. She was my cat companion for almost sixteen years and would check on me when I was up late in the kitchen and tell me to go to bed when the night grew long.

RECIPE INDEX

A

C

E

H

I

J

K

M

N

V

W

Y

ANIME INDEX

H

I

J

K

L

M

N

P

R

T

U

V

W

X

Y

ABOUT THE AUTHOR

Born in Germany and raised on an old family farm in Virginia, **Diana Ault** has been conducting kitchen experiments and watching anime since she was very young. She began her blog, *Fiction-Food Café*, focusing on food found in books, movies, TV shows, and video games, in early 2013. Her recipes have been included in *Easy Eats: A Bee and Puppycat Cookbook*; the *Hyrule: Taste of the Wild* fanzine; *The Dragon Prince Recipe Zine*; *PokéCafé: A Pokémon Café Food Fanzine*; and in the FanMail subscription box. Diana currently resides in Germany with her husband and daughter.